MW01181172

Central Texas
⇒ T A L E S ⇐

Central Texas
T A L E S

M I K E C O X

THE
History
PRESS

Published by The History Press
Charleston, SC 29403
www.historypress.net

Copyright © 2012 by Mike Cox
All rights reserved

First published 2012

ISBN 978.154.0232212

Library of Congress CIP data applied for.

Contents

CONTENTS

CONTENTS

INTRODUCTION

T hough born in Amarillo up on the Caprock in the Texas Panhandle, I grew up down state in Austin, which is the center city of Central Texas. Of course, Austin's also the state capital, but that's another story.

Central Texas Tales is a collection of fifty-two stories about the history, people and places of the middle of Texas, that area from the Hill Country on the west to the green farmland on the east. By my geography, the area runs north to Waco, beyond which I consider North Texas. To the south, Central Texas extends through New Braunfels, below which there is San Antonio and the beginning of South Texas.

The area is as diverse culturally as it is geographically. Part of my roots trace to the German immigrants who settled the Hill Country town of Fredericksburg in the mid-1840s. But only thirty miles east of Austin is Bastrop, which with its stand of Lost Pines (though badly impacted by a terrible 2011 wildfire) is more like East Texas than Central Texas. And back on the other side of Austin, places like Llano and Mason are on the cusp of being more like West Texas than Central Texas.

One thing, at least in a year when a normal amount of precipitation has fallen over the area, ties all the counties of Central Texas together: the bluebonnet. In early spring in non-drought times, the sweet-smelling wildflower—Texas's state flower—can be found in profusion across the entire area. In fact, if this part of Texas ever felt the need for a nickname, it easily could be Bluebonnet Country.

While one of the smaller geographic regions of the state, Central Texas has grown tremendously in population. Austin has gone from being a medium-sized college and government town in the 1970s to, at last ranking, the thirteenth-largest city in the nation and fourth-largest in Texas. The growth has brought considerable change to the area, not all for the better, considering the loss of native habitat for wildlife and frequent bumper-to-bumper traffic in Austin. On the plus side, a lot of people, and the passage of nearly two centuries since the area saw its first settlement by Anglos, translates into the potential for a lot of stories.

Given that, this anthology, the fourth in a series of books based on my weekly "Texas Tales" newspaper column, easily could have been three times as long as it is. But while there is no shortage of good stories to tell, the maximum size of the titles in this series is finite.

That said, I've tried to pick the most interesting stories I know about this part of Texas, and I hope you'll enjoy reading them.

INDIANS

SARAH'S STORY

"Son," a wise old man once said, "always marry a Texas girl. No matter what happens, she's seen worse."

Few Texas women ever saw any worse than Sarah Creath McSherry Hibbens Stinnett Howard. A woman with true grit and more, the way she came by her long name is one of Texas's more gripping tales.

She was born Sarah Creath on January 7, 1810, in Jackson County, Illinois, where her prosperous family ran a large plantation. Her mother died when she was two, but her father soon remarried. Maybe she had a difficult relationship with her mother or simply an appetite for adventure. Whatever the reason, Sarah seems to have had no trouble letting go of the figurative apron strings of home.

Described as "a beautiful blonde…[who was] graceful in manner and pure of heart," at only seventeen Sarah married one John McSherry, described by historians as an industrious, hardworking Irishman. Not much is known about the young couple's life in Illinois, but in 1828, they came to Texas and settled in Green DeWitt's colony along the Guadalupe River.

McSherry built them a log cabin on Little Carlisle Creek, about two hundred yards from a good spring. As one writer later put it, "They were happily devoted to each other." In 1833, on Sarah's twenty-third birthday, five years after they settled in the Mexican province of Texas, their son was

Her beauty belying her grit, Sarah Howard lost two husbands and a child to the Comanches. *Author's collection.*

born. (Other accounts have the birth occurring in 1829, but the latter date is based on more recent research.)

Around noon one day, McSherry grabbed a bucket and walked to the spring for water. A few moments later, Sarah heard her husband scream. Holding her baby, she opened their cabin door and ventured outside just far enough to see that he was being attacked by Indians. As she looked on in horror, they killed and then scalped him.

Running back inside, she barred the door and stood ready with her husband's rifle, fully prepared to drive off the Indians. For some reason, the Indians opted not to attack and left. A neighbor happened by later that night and took the young widow and her child to safety.

Sarah and her little boy lived with neighbor Andrew Lockhart and his family for a time before she found a new husband, John Hibbens. In the summer of 1835, Sarah—who by then had a child by Hibbens—traveled with her two children to Illinois to visit her family.

When she returned to Texas early in 1836, she was accompanied by her only brother, George. Hibbens met them with an ox cart at Columbia, not far up the Brazos from the coast, and the five of them began their trek back to the Guadalupe Valley. Fifteen miles from their home, in present Lavaca County, they were attacked by Comanches. The Indians killed Hibbens and

Creath and took Sarah and her two children captive. Riding northwest, the raiders headed toward the High Plains with their captives. The second day out, tiring of Sarah's crying infant, the Indians killed it by smashing its head against a tree.

Not longer after they reached present Travis County, a strong norther blew in. The Indians made camp on the south side of a cedar brake to wait out the harsh weather. On the third night at this camp, Sarah lay awake as her captors slept and thought about how she could escape. Knowing she could not travel with her son, she made the excruciatingly hard decision to leave him behind while she went for help. Wrapping him in a buffalo robe, she slipped away into the cold darkness.

Late the following day, a company of Texas Rangers sat around their fire about to eat their supper when a nearly nude, bleeding and bruised woman staggered into their camp. After hearing Sarah's story, the men left Sarah with a family who lived nearby, saddled up and rode off in pursuit of the Indians. The next day, after a hard ride and a harder fight with the Indians, they succeeded in rescuing the child.

That summer, the twice-widowed Sarah married again, this time taking former neighbor Claiborne Stinnett as her husband. They moved to Stinnett's land in Gonzales County, where Stinnett later briefly served as sheriff. Two years later, Stinnett vanished after leaving on a business trip for Linnville, a coastal community near present Port Lavaca. At first, everyone thought he had met the same fate as Sarah's first two husbands. But in 1842, four years after Stinnett's disappearance, two runaway slaves found in Mexico confessed that they had robbed and killed him and described where his remains could be found.

Only twenty-five, Sarah had outlived three husbands, her only brother and one of her children, all of them having died violently. It took only a short time before a fourth man, a twenty-five-year-old Kentuckian named Phillip Howard, decided to take a chance on marrying Sarah. The couple tied the knot in May 1839 and eventually settled in Bosque County. Thirty-one mostly good years passed before death again ended a marriage for Sarah. This time, though, she was the one who died—of natural causes.

The year was 1870, making her about sixty when she left Howard a widower. She had lived in Texas for more than forty years, but not long enough to see the end of the Indian wars in her adopted state that had cost her so dearly. Another eight years would go by before Rangers tangled with Comanches for the last time in 1878, and in January 1881, Texans had their final fight with the Apaches in far West Texas.

Sarah's last husband eventually married a woman named Rebecca. About seven years younger than her new husband, she and Howard were together until his death on January 6, 1894. His family buried him in the Meridian Cemetery, where, only a little more than a month later, Rebecca joined him in a state more enduring than any marriage.

Descendants who have delved into Sarah's story believe she is buried in the old Fort Graham Cemetery near Lake Whitney in Bosque County. A thorough search of the cemetery has failed to turn up a tombstone bearing her name, but several of the older graves have illegible markers. One of those could be Sarah's.

Maybe Thomas Rusk, once the Republic of Texas's secretary of war, had Sarah's trying life in mind when he said, "The men of Texas deserved much credit, but more was due the women. Armed men facing a foe could not but be brave; but the women, with their little children around them, without means of defense or power to resist, faced danger and death with unflinching courage."

Few Texas women ever had a better claim than Sarah Creath McSherry Hibbens Stinnett Howard of being one tough lady.

PSYCHOLOGICAL WARFARE ON THE FRONTIER

"Psychological operations," the U.S. military term for playing mind games on the enemy, is not a new concept. The only difference between modern psychological warfare and the past is that it is more sophisticated these days. Officers and soldiers are now formally trained in tactics ranging from annoying the enemy by playing loud music to dropping thousands of propaganda leaflets from aircraft. Back when the U.S. Army bore responsibility for protecting Texas's frontier from hostile Indians, the technique was much more informal.

The Fort Mason chloroform caper is a good example of nineteenth-century "psych ops." Established in 1851 on a hill in what is now the county seat town of Mason, Fort Mason lay well into Comanche country. Soldiers spent far more time peeling potatoes and currying their horses than fighting Indians, but the Indians remained an ongoing concern, preying on settlers or travelers whenever they got a chance. But a little out-of-the-box thinking certainly calmed things down for a time.

One of the officers stationed at the fort was Lafayette Guild, the post surgeon. When he received a shipment of chloroform, a chemical that only recently had been proven to have value as an anesthetic, he had an idea.

The doctor went to Colonel Charles A. May, an officer of the Second Dragoons, and got his buy-in to the plan. The post commander also gave his approval.

When one band of Indians agreed to a powwow, the six-foot, four-inch, two-hundred-pound May had himself introduced to the Indians as a powerful medicine man. His medicine ran so strong, Dr. Guild told the Indians, that he could bring the dead back to life.

The big colonel stood up next to the fire. If any of the Indians would like to volunteer, the colonel said, he would gladly demonstrate his powers. When none of the Indians attending the council stepped forward, May scooped up a small dog and said it would do. May left with the dog under his arm and went inside his tent to work his medicine. Once out of sight, as instructed by Dr. Guild, the colonel put the dog temporarily to sleep with a strong whiff of chloroform.

Carrying the apparently dead dog back to the circle of Indians and military officers, May made a big show of demonstrating his gifts. The Indians were

Fort Mason stood on a high hill overlooking the town that bore its name. *Photo by the author.*

not too impressed until the colonel drew a knife and began cutting off the dog's tail a piece at a time. When the dog showed no signs of noticing that he was being de-tailed, the Indians began to look more interested. For good measure, May handed each chief in the band a piece of the tail. Then he said he would bring the dog back to life.

The colonel carried the freshly bob-tailed feist back to his tent and waited until it came to. When the officer returned to the campfire, the barking dog followed him, clearly alive and well, albeit suffering from a sore behind.

For the rest of Colonel May's tour at Fort Mason, relations with the Indians were decidedly pacific. The chiefs who attended the council carried their piece of dog tail in their medicine pouches for a long time, and the dog that had undergone a field amputation went about his life not caring that he had a shorter tail than he started with. And anytime a soldier or settler needed a broken bone set or surgery, Dr. Guild used chloroform to keep them from feeling pain.

STEVEN WILLIAMSON'S LOST GRAVE

The army, both in its absence and its presence, has had a big impact on Coryell County over the years. The establishment of Fort Gates on the Leon River in 1849 is what helped stimulate settlement of the area as folks in Bell, Burleson, Milam and Washington Counties began to move into the eastern and southern parts of Coryell County. Hostile Indians wisely steered clear of the vicinity.

The military abandoned the stockaded garrison (one of the few Hollywood-style military posts ever actually built in Texas) in March 1852, but the settlers drawn by the protection the army had offered did not. By the 1860s, some of the county's early settlers had moved westward, building cabins near what soon became the community of Pearl.

With the soldiers gone and most of Texas's fighting men tied up in the Civil War, the Comanches felt free to raid all along the state's western frontier. Texas's Confederate state government fielded companies of Rangers to patrol the outlying counties, but they couldn't be everywhere at once.

That's how things stood on April 26, 1863, when a Comanche raiding party came upon a settler named Steven Williamson, who lived several miles southeast of Pearl. When Williamson didn't come home that night, worried family and friends saddled up to look for him. They found his arrow-studded body lying near a large tree that he may have tried to use for cover. The Indians had scalped him and then pinned his thighs together, a sign that he had defended himself gamely. Likely he wounded or killed some of his attackers before they overpowered him. His family carried his body home in the back of an ox-drawn wagon, built a coffin, lined it with black calico and took him to the southern part of the county near the settlement of Eliga for burial.

Years later, Gordon Shook, Williamson's great-grandson, could still identify the live oak where his relative had been killed and posed for a photograph there. Charles E. Freeman used the image in his book, *A History of Pearl, Texas*. Gordon Williamson's grandfather, J.W. Shook, in 1875 had settled the land where the attack had occurred. Freeman also included in his book a couple of accounts from Coryell County old-timers who lived through those bloody days.

Mrs. W.W. Robinson remembered a time when she was a little girl and she and her father just missed a run-in with Comanches. During the week, she and her brother John stayed at her uncle Andy Bone's place on Cowhouse Creek so they could attend a one-room school at King. One Friday, her father, Eli Williamson (whether he was related to the late Steven Williamson was not mentioned in the book), came to pick them up for the weekend. Her brother rode his own horse while she sat behind her father on his horse. Not far from their home on Beehouse Creek, her father spotted a group of Indians before the Indians saw them. Yelling for his daughter to hang on, Williamson wheeled his horse and galloped off in the opposite direction. They made it home safely, but Mrs. Robinson never forgot that scary ride.

Coryell County residents continued to stay alert for prowling Indians for several years more. Dallas Edmondson later told of a Comanche horse-stealing foray down Beehouse Creek in 1871. The Indians missed his horses, which he had out grazing, but they made off with many others.

Though he died violently, Steven Williamson's body rested in peace until World War II broke out and the army decided to return to Coryell and surrounding counties. This time, of course, the military wasn't moving in to protect residents from hostile Indians. The army needed a lot of open land for tank and artillery training.

The army bought thousands of acres, including the area where Williamson had been buried. Some three hundred families had to give up their land and move. Any grave on the soon-to-be military reservation that could be located was dug up and the remains reinterred, but even with the help of surviving family members, Williamson's burial site could not be found. Its location remains unknown today.

The Civil War

The Battle of Bull Creek

Now covered with spacious, expensive houses, the cedar-studded canyons on the western edge of Austin used to be Central Texas's version of Appalachia. Remote and hard to reach in the days of horse and wagon travel, the hills west of the Capital City were peopled by scattered families who came from the mountains of Tennessee and Kentucky and settled there because the terrain reminded them of home. But not all of these families hailed from the South. The Will Preece clan had come to Texas from Illinois, and when Southerners started talking about leaving the Union, the Preeces brooked no interest in the concept. In fact, old man Preece's cousin was Thomas Lincoln, father of the man recently elected president.

That set of circumstances led to a long-forgotten series of gunfights and ambushes in the hills of Travis County, a Civil War conflict for which no historical markers stand in commemoration. Texas's Battle of Bull Creek hardly compares with the Battle of Bull Run, but the partisan feelings that triggered the fight ran as deep.

Generally lost in most Civil War stories is the fact that not everyone in the South, particularly in Texas, favored secession. In fact, Travis County voted to stay in the Union.

The late Harold Preece, a Travis County native who heard the stories from his father and other relatives, wrote a slightly fictionalized account of the Battle of Bull Creek for a long-defunct pulp western magazine, *Real West*.

Preece intended to include the story in an autobiography, but his book never made it to print.

The first movement in the battle came shortly after the secession election results became known. A squad of Confederate recruitment officers, "flushed with good bourbon and electoral victory," rode into the hills to enlist "mountain cowboys" for the CSA cavalry.

As the Rebels approached Will Preece's cabin, which stood in the vicinity of Bull Creek, a rifle bullet cut the bridle of one of the riders. A second shot from another of the Preece family removed the eyebrow hair from another secessionist. More lead followed, but none of the Rebels caught any. Since the Preeces provisioned their larder with deer and squirrel they shot, the misses may have been intentional—mere warning shots.

The riders turned and rode back to Austin. Four months would go by before the bombardment of Fort Sumter, but the Civil War had started in Texas.

That June—Preece did not give the day—twenty Travis County Unionists calling themselves the Mountain Eagles ambushed more than twice that number of Confederate cavalrymen on their way to the pro-Union German settlements farther west. The half-hour gun battle near Martin's Well claimed nine "Secesh," as the hill men called the Southerners. Another six men suffered wounds.

This early postcard of Bull Creek emphasizes its scenic beauty, not the ugly Civil War fight that happened there. *Author's collection.*

In response, the governor commissioned a special Ranger company to root out the pro-Union element west of Austin. The Southern partisans scoured the hills, giving young men the choice of conscription in the Confederate army or a permanent draft deferment at the end of a rope. Those considered incorrigible did not get the military service option.

By January 1, 1862, only forty of the Mountain Eagles remained in the hills. Their ammunition supply low, the men had holed up in a makeshift piled-stone fortress atop a prominence offering a good view of all approaches. Opting not to celebrate New Year's Day, state forces attacked the Unionist stronghold. Preece wrote that his uncle claimed thirty Secesh and three Unionists died in the battle near Bull Creek but admitted that "half that number for Confederates and double that figure for the Eagles would probably be a less biased estimate." In truth, the numbers likely came to even fewer than that or else the battle site would have been better remembered. But the location of the fort did come to be called Dead Man's Peak.

The fight ended the mini-war in the hills west of the Capital City. The surviving Mountain Eagles rode to Mexico, and four of the Preeces ended up in New Orleans. After the war, their loyalty to the Union never having wavered, they returned to Bull Creek.

SHROPSHIRE'S CASTLE

Writing by candlelight, Captain John Shropshire scratched out another letter to his beloved Carrie. The captain and his fellow Confederate soldiers had covered nearly twelve miles that November day in 1861, stopping to make camp on the Frio River about sixty miles from Fort Clark.

The Central Texas boys from Columbus were on their way to El Paso and eventually New Mexico. Shropshire knew it would be a long time before he held his wife in his arms again or saw their son, Charlie. "If peace is not declared before we leave [El Paso], we can not possibly get back before 12 mo…which to me appears an age to be separated from my family," he wrote.

Shropshire had been writing his wife since August, when his company marched off to war. "I tell you," he had written, "soldiering so far has not been the most pleasant occupation I have followed."

Indeed, before the war, he had been a successful cotton farmer. "But these are no times to long for the comforts of home," he continued.

Columbus's old water tower didn't always look like a castle turret, but it's been around a long time. *Author's collection.*

Early in the campaign, he had at least eaten well. "I managed to eat or worry down a small portion of a calf and also a pig which we pressed into the service of the Southern Confederacy," he wrote.

"The candle has burnt out and I am writing by moonlight," Shropshire continued in his November missive. "The moon shines very brightly in this country."

By early December, Shropshire wrote Carrie that his company was "dirty and hungry all the time."

The day after Christmas, Shropshire wrote from a camp near the Rio Grande not far from Fort Quitman. Fighting Yankees would come, but for the time being, West Texas had proven a formidable adversary in its own right. "I candidly confess I never would have come this way had I imagined the country was so mean," Shropshire wrote. "If I had the Yankeys at my disposal I would given them this country and force them to live in it. I would make Devil's River hollow headquarters for them."

By late January 1862, the Texans had reached New Mexico. "In this long wearisome march my fancy has been idle and allowed to roam at will," he penned. "Many are the fancy castles I have built for you and I and our little ones and I believe that some of them will be realized."

Shropshire finally saw a fight coming, but he worried more about Carrie than himself. "Remember darling," he wrote, "that if I am so unfortunate as to number among the slain in our country's cause that to you alone on earth will our children have to depend."

When the smoke cleared after the Battle of Glorietta Pass, Shropshire indeed lay among the unfortunate who would never see Texas again. Though he never got to build his wife that "fancy castle" he had dreamed about, his name did eventually become associated with a structure reminiscent of one.

A round, white tower on the Colorado County courthouse square in the center of Columbus looks like an architectural survivor of the days of yore in England. No matter how European it looks, however, the tower is the product of Yankee—well, Southern—ingenuity.

In the spring of 1883, two decades after the war that claimed Shropshire, a fire gutted a livery stable and adjoining hotel in Columbus. Volunteer firefighters managed to contain the blaze before it leveled downtown, but getting enough water on the fire had been a problem. To provide a clearly needed water system, the city fathers authorized construction of a sturdy water tower. Built by R.J. Jones, the two-story tower took shape from 400,000 locally made bricks. With walls nearly three feet thick, the tower supported a substantial metal water tank on its top. Beneath it, the city's volunteer fire department had its office and equipment.

According to the late Bill Stein, longtime Columbus librarian and historian, while the city built the tower, it stood on county property. When the city government was dissolved for a time in 1906, no one thought of formally transferring the tower to the county. Even so, when a hurricane damaged the top of the tower in 1909, the county had the structure repaired. But three years later, county officials decided the city needed a better water system. With completion of that system, the brick tower stood abandoned.

In 1926, it finally occurred to someone that the old tower had other than utilitarian value. The officers of the John Shropshire and John C. Upton chapter of the United Daughters of the Confederacy (UDC) got county officials to agree to let them use the tower as their meeting place.

When the city was reinstituted in 1927, the municipal government evidently reclaimed the tower. Shortly afterward, the city hired someone to tear the tower down. When the UDC saw part of the old tower falling (it was not as indestructible as legend holds), they ran over to see the mayor and got the demolition stopped. Local architect Milton Wirtz and contractor A.N. Evans Sr. refurbished the structure, adding a small, rounded room on the east side of its base, a long, narrow window and a circular staircase leading to the second floor. The tower's castle-like crenellation is not an original feature but merely the architect's clever way of covering the damage done during the aborted razing of the structure.

In 1962, the old water tower became the home of Columbus's Confederate Memorial Museum and Veterans Hall. A photograph of Shropshire hangs on the museum wall, and his letters have been saved for posterity by Columbus's Nesbitt Memorial Library.

CONFEDERATE VETS DIDN'T FIND JULY 4 PARTICULARLY EXCITING

One year before the American Centennial, most of the nation heartily celebrated the signing of the Declaration of Independence on Sunday, July 4, 1875.

Three days later, on Wednesday, July 7, only a decade after the bloody Civil War that nearly made moot what happened in Philadelphia in 1776, the surviving members of Terry's Texas Rangers gathered at Austin's Barton Springs for a reunion. Though popularly known as Terry's Texas Rangers, the command organized in Houston in 1861 by B.F. Terry and T.S. Lubbock was officially the Eighth Texas Cavalry. They were regular gray-clad soldiers, not Indian-fighting Texas Rangers. Still, some of them had ridden as Rangers before the war.

So why didn't the ex-Confederates have their get-together on Sunday after church rather than wait until the middle of the workweek? Was it simply a matter of scheduling, or were those battle-scarred Rebels who had their annual meeting in the Capital City that year still somewhat unreconstructed?

A reunion badge worn by former Terry's Texas Ranger E.H. McKnight. *Author's collection.*

The account of the event published in the *Austin Daily Statesman* did not address the calendar issue, but it's not hard to imagine that men who had fought hard for the South and lost many friends in the process still had a little trouble getting too fired up over the Fourth of July.

The Texans who rode with Terry and Lubbock, and later under Colonel John A. Wharton, paid a high price for their beliefs. Of 1,700 who served in the regiment, the Eighth Texas consisted of only 150 men by the end of the war. "Many of them died from exposure and disease, many were killed in battle, many were seriously wounded and forced to retire from the service, and many became prisoners of war," the *Confederate Veteran* magazine later noted, "but it is said that no one of them ever deserted the cause. They were the… swiftest horsemen, the surest and best shots, and of the coolest and bravest… [unit] that ever charged a battery."

No matter why the veterans set July 7 rather than July 4 as their meeting date, they had a fine time along Barton Creek that afternoon. "The weather was warm," the newspaper reported, "but the surroundings of the place are so delightful that this objection was to a great extent overcome. The clear, limpid, dashing stream added its cheerfulness to the scene while soldierly hands once more clasped each other in brotherly affection."

Though Barton Springs had long been a popular venue for picnics and other outdoor activities, the adjacent land was then private property. The Confederate veterans met under the pecan trees on land belonging to fellow former Rebel William C. Walsh, who owned a nearby quarry.

Captain Rufus King, the ranking surviving officer of the regiment, called the reunion to order at noon. Early in the war, King had raised a company in Bastrop County and eventually became the senior captain in the regiment. The newspaper filled in the rest of his service record: "He remained with the Rangers until the battle of Shiloh, where he received three balls in his body, one passing through his shoulders, another shivering in his arm and the third spending itself in his thigh." After King spoke, he asked another veteran to offer the invocation. Following the prayer, the captain called the roll. Sixty veterans answered present.

The highest-ranking former Confederate on hand at Barton Springs that hot afternoon was General Braxton Bragg, a North Carolinian, 1837 West Point graduate and Mexican War veteran then working as a railroad inspector in Galveston. The namesake of future Fort Bragg, home of the Eighty-second Airborne Division, Bragg had been one of only eight general officers to lead Confederate forces during what some sons of the South call the War of Northern Aggression.

While not the Confederacy's brightest star, for a time Bragg stood at the top of the chain of command of the Eighth Texas. Known by historians as a well-organized if sometimes incompetent sourpuss, Bragg had been asked to speak to the Texans. "Like a soldier...[he] obeyed," the *Statesman* reported. The article continued: "His remarks were on the style of 'a little more grape' [as in "have another drink, boys"], and were enthusiastically received by his hearers. His towering form, noble demeanor, suavity and age, are such as to command the respect of any one."

Barely a year later, just fifty-nine years old, Bragg dropped dead while walking with a friend down the street in Galveston. His body was shipped to Mobile, Alabama, for burial, but some say his spirit remains in Texas in the form of an apparition known as Bragg's Light.

As many of the former Rebels meeting at Barton Springs followed Bragg's "order" and enjoyed distilled spirits or cold brew, regimental chaplain R.S. Bunting closed out the formalities with a reading of another officer's order—the April 30, 1865 swan song of General "Fighting" Joseph Wheeler, commander of the corps that included Terry's Texas Rangers:

> *Gallant Comrades—You have fought your fight: your task is done. During a four years' struggle for liberty you have exhibited courage, fortitude and devotion. You are the victors of more than two hundred sternly contested fields. You have participated in more than one thousand conflicts of arms. You are heroes! Veterans! Patriots! The bones of your comrades mark battle fields upon the soil of Kentucky, Tennessee, Virginia, North Carolina, South Carolina, Georgia, Alabama and Mississippi. You have done all that human exertions could accomplish.*

LAW AND DISORDER

TWO GRAVES FILLED IN THE NAME OF HONOR

A lot of men—and a few bold women—came to Texas for reasons that had nothing to do with a simple desire to see some new country. Some found that while they might escape bad debt, an empty marriage or an arrest warrant, they could not outride their own character. But splashing across the Sabine or Red River made them a Texan, for better or worse.

One man who rode into Texas with little more than a pair of saddlebags and a reputation was Colonel Junius Henry. His story's back trail led all the way east to Florida. During the Seminole War in the early 1830s, the colonel in command of a noted regiment received a letter from his wife in Augusta, Georgia, that said she was about to have their baby. In the polite parlance of the day, she was "on the eve of confinement." He left Florida immediately to be at her bedside.

The next day, his unit took part in a particularly tough fight with the Indians. Not long after that, the colonel's hometown newspaper carried an article suggesting that his hasty departure from the field had more to do with him wanting to save his scalp than concern for his wife.

One of the colonel's staff officers, a captain who also happened to be his brother, rode to Augusta to find the person behind the printed attack on his kin. The newspaper editor, doubtless under pressure and possibly at pistol point, revealed that the source for the article was one of the generals participating in the campaign. That man also was from Augusta.

The southern tradition of dueling sent many men to early graves. *Author's collection.*

Unknown to Captain Henry, another of the colonel's officers also had traveled to Augusta to seek satisfaction—the gentlemanly term for challenging someone to a duel—with the offending general. The general responded to Captain Henry's demand by saying that as soon as he took care of the other captain, he would be happy to discuss the matter with him as well. In short order, somewhere in the vicinity of Augusta, the general mortally wounded the first captain in a Bowie knife duel. Pistols were agreed on as the weapon for the second duel, a contest the general also won.

With two men already dead over a foolhardy sense of honor, Henry went to Augusta to avenge the death of his brother. Not bothering with the formality of a duel, he found the general in a hotel and opened fire as soon as he saw him. The gunfight left the general seriously wounded and Colonel Henry lacking a third finger, the digit removed by the general's bullet. Not slowed by the wound to his hand, Henry lit into the general with a Bowie knife. Bystanders finally separated the two, but Henry vowed he would kill the general the next time he saw him.

Three months later, the general having recovered, Henry went looking for him with a double-barreled shotgun. The buckshot tamped down in one of the barrels included a slug that had been cut from his dead brother's body. This time, the general's luck ran out. When Henry found him, he unloaded the scatter gun on the offending officer. The first blast removed his shoulder. The second sent lead through his heart.

After the encounter, Colonel Henry found it expedient to leave Georgia for Texas. Not long after his arrival in the young republic, he ran into a man who made some disparaging remarks concerning Henry's role in the Augusta vendetta. The result was another dead man, but Henry had been seriously wounded and soon died.

An account of this feud, and its final act in Texas, was published in a long-extinct Atlanta newspaper in 1875. Unfortunately, the writer deemed it best that he not use the real names of the participants. Maybe he did it out of feelings for the relatives of the combatants. Maybe he figured if he used actual names, someone might come around gunning for him in retaliation for his having opened old wounds. Neither does the story say where in Texas Colonel Henry died for having taken up for his slain brother.

"This feud, involving the death of so many superb men and bankrupting two powerful families," the newspaper said, "is but one of a thousand that might be traced through the system of Southern society."

WALDRIP'S WOLFPACK: THE HANGERBANDE

Whether James P. Waldrip did what he did out of loyalty to the South or just because he possessed a serious mean streak may never be known. Whatever his motivation, the Hill Country is sprinkled with the graves of pro-Union Germans that the Gillespie County farmer helped to fill.

Those who immigrated to Texas from Germany in the mid-1840s almost universally opposed secession and the Civil War that followed in 1861. When the Confederate government passed a conscription law in April 1862 requiring that every male in the South from age seventeen to thirty-five (a year later, the age ceiling went to fifty) pledge allegiance to the Confederacy and serve in its army, the friction between the Southerners and pro-Unionists soon turned violent.

On August 10, 1862, along the Nueces River in South Texas, Confederate troops attacked the camp of sixty-one pro-Unionists attempting to flee to Mexico. They killed nineteen men, mostly German intellectuals, and wounded nine others who were soon summarily executed. That fall, eight more Germans were killed on the Rio Grande as they tried to cross to the other side. Violence against Union sympathizers continued periodically throughout the war across the state, though the massacre on the Nueces stood as the worst instance.

Early Fredericksburg street scene. *Author's collection.*

In the Hill Country, Waldrip led a gang that came to be known as Waldrip's Wolfpack or simply the Hangerbande (the hanging band). Waldrip and his men dragged schoolteacher Louis Schuetze from his house in Fredericksburg around sundown on February 24, 1864. Paying no attention to his cries of, "Think of my wife and children!" a party of fifteen to twenty men took the young family man to a tree about three miles north of town and hanged him.

At the coroner's inquest, Schuetze's daughter testified that she saw her father taken from their house. "I heard a blow," she continued, "and my father cried out 'Mr. Waldrip' and then 'Louise, come here.' I tore myself loose and hurried to my father. 'My Louisa,' he said, 'they are going to hang me.'"

The justice of the peace who conducted the inquest said Schuetze had been found hanging from "a bough of a live oak. His hands were bound behind his back. On the left side of his forehead a wound was found. His pockets were turned inside out."

On March 9, 1864, Waldrip and his gang visited the home of William Fellers, who lived in the Gillespie County community of Grapetown. Fellers, his wife, Clara, and their four daughters were eating supper when Waldrip and his cohorts took him away. The next day, Mrs. Fellers learned that her husband and two of their neighbors had been hanged.

Shortly after Confederate Brigadier General John D. McAdoo arrived in Fredericksburg on June 23, 1864, he reported: "I found almost the entire population…laboring under the greatest excitement. Within a few months, twenty men had perished by violence. Some had been waylaid and shot; others taken from their homes at the dead hour of midnight and hung, and their houses robbed…No man felt secure—even at home. The Indians seemed to be the least talked of, the least thought of, and the least dreaded of all the evils that threatened and afflicted the Frontier."

No one knows how many pro-Union Germans Waldrip had a hand in hanging. Some estimates hold that as many as 150 Germans died in the Hill Country during the war. Whatever the number, Waldrip and his followers killed more white men in that part of Central Texas than Indian war parties ever did.

A few of Waldrip's cohorts did get arrested and tried by civil authorities, but Waldrip could never be found. He had left the area, possibly riding south to Mexico. But in 1867, he made the mistake of returning to Fredericksburg. By then, as he was either too arrogant or too stupid to appreciate, those of Germanic heritage had regained firm control of their county. Someone in town spotted the hated Waldrip and shouted an alert, and the chase was on.

James P. Waldrip died under this tree that still stands on North Washington Street in downtown Fredericksburg. *Courtesy Ann Baltzer.*

Bertha Nimitz, daughter of the Hotel Nimitz's proprietors, saw Waldrip trying to hide near the well in the courtyard behind her family's inn on the town's wide main street. She told the pursuers where they could find him, and as one account put it, "soon a shot felled him outside the hotel court wall." As other bullets thudded into him, he is said to have cried out, "Oh God, please don't shoot any more!"

Another version of Waldrip's demise has one Henry Langerham shooting Waldrip "like a turkey," putting a bullet between his eyes. However the one-time gang leader's moment of retribution played out, Waldrip did not survive. The consensus among historians is that he died beneath a large live oak that still grows adjacent to the old Nimitz barn, now part of the National Museum of the Pacific War.

Waldrip's vigilante-style executioners unceremoniously buried him on the bank of nearby Baron's Creek, on property now occupied by the Fredericksburg Inn and Suites about a block and a half south of the Nimitz. Before they closed his hastily dug grave, someone tossed in his black beaver hat. Animals dug into Waldrip's grave a short time later, and he had to be reburied. The creek is prone to flooding, so there's no telling where his bones ended up.

Needless to say, no tombstone marks his final resting place.

DEAD MAN'S HOLE

The expression "he simply dropped out of sight" had both figurative and literal meaning in Burnet County during and after the Civil War. Common belief held that folks who disappeared in that area often ended up at the bottom of a 150-plus-foot-deep limestone fissure south of Marble Falls called Dead Man's Hole. Local lore has it that the bodies of as many as seventeen men were tossed down the hole. Some hapless souls may have been thrown in while they were still alive.

The first person of European descent to the see the hole up close had better luck than many subsequent visitors—he lived to tell the tale. Ferdinand Lueders, a German naturalist, noted his discovery of the feature in 1821 while passing through the area looking for unusual insects. Nearly a quarter of a century would go by before settlers began building cabins in the area and rediscovered the hole.

During the Civil War, Central Texas proved a dangerous place for those who didn't cotton to secession. Unionists, as they came to be called, found

Dead Man's Hole today isn't much deeper than a hot tub, but originally it went 150 feet down. *Photo by the author.*

themselves on the open-season list. Some of them, according to once-whispered stories, ended up at the bottom of Dead Man's Hole. Despite the claim that the hole proved to be the final destination of as many as seventeen men, local historians have come up with only five names, and two of those are speculative.

The best-known Dead Man's Hole disappearee is Benjamin McKeever. Described as a "dashing...swain" full of southern (read racist) pride, one day in August 1872, McKeever fired shots at a dog snapping at his horse's heels. He missed his target several times and also missed when he fired a round at the dog's owner. The owner was an African American man, which in that era tended to mean that local authorities would not be overly concerned about pursuing any charges against McKeever. The dog owner's friends, however, took umbrage to the assault and ambushed McKeever a few days later. When they unloaded shotguns in his direction, they did not miss.

As soon as McKeever's friends realized he was missing, a search party rode out to check Dead Man's Hole, as the formation already had a reputation as something of a limestone tomb. Sure enough, someone spotted a blanket and shoe known to have belonged to McKeever hanging on a ledge partway down the dark hole. With some effort, volunteers pulled McKeever's body up from the bottom, though accumulated gases in the fissure caused the sheriff to pass out.

Three of five men subsequently indicted for murder in McKeever's death later received life sentences. The fourth defendant got a two-year prison term, and the fifth seems to have been found not guilty.

As Burnet County became more law-abiding, Dead Man's Hole fell from usage. But as time passed, people began telling stories of its dark past. It became the most haunted venue in the area.

Because of gases that tended to build up in the hole, it remained unexplored until 1951, when breathing equipment could be used. The Texas Speleological Society mapped the feature in 1968, measuring it as 155 feet deep and extending 50 feet in length.

In 1999, landowner Ona Lou Roper deeded Burnet County 6.5 acres around the hole for use as a park. A year earlier, a state historical marker had been put up at the site. The opening to the hole had been sealed with a heavy metal grate for years, but later that was removed and the feature mostly filled with caliche.

Is Dead Man's Hole haunted by seventeen restless souls forced to drop from sight before their time? One website that reports news of the supernatural says that amateur ghost hunters have detected Class-A EVPs in the vicinity of the feature. EVP is ghost hunter talk for electronic voice phenomena. They are voices, according to another website on the subject of ghost detecting, "that you can understand, and [that] can be heard by most all people over a speaker or headphone." A human voice is capable of a frequency range from 300 Hz to 3000 Hz; EVPs are "voices" logging in below 300 Hz or above 3000 Hz.

"The energy out there is so strong that we couldn't get the video equipment to keep a charge for even five minutes," one investigator who visited Dead Man's Hole later said, "and our full pack of batteries had been drained before we ever got to use them. They hadn't even been taken out of the package."

Voices or no voices, few could argue that Dead Man's Hole is not an aptly named landmark.

HOLD THE PRESS FOR A HANGING

Until 1923, when the state began using the electric chair, Texas judges sometimes signed off on a different kind of "suspended sentence"—hanging by the neck until dead. Texas sheriffs once had the responsibility of conducting executions at the county level. Legal hangings didn't happen every day, so when one came up, it usually made for big news.

Forty years ago, the late Edmunds Travis of Austin recalled a hanging he reluctantly covered for the Austin daily he worked for in 1913.

For decades, Austin had a red-light district where prostitution was tolerated literally within the limits. The zone extended from Colorado Street on the east to San Antonio Street on the west and from Second Street on the south to the alley between Fourth and Fifth Streets on the north. Folks called it Guy Town.

In 1913, a well-known barkeep who worked in the district got "run in" for shooting one of the damsels of the demimonde in the back of the head. The Capital City then being a small town, the killing made for big news. Police said the man had quarreled with one of the girls before shooting her. The bartender maintained he and the "lady" had indeed argued but the fatal outcome amounted only to an accident. He said he had merely meant to prod her in the back of the head with the barrel of his six-shooter. Unfortunately, the pistol had discharged.

A jury chose to believe the state's version of the story and found the bartender guilty of murder. The judge sentenced him to hang. As the condemned man's last day approached, the Travis County sheriff printed and distributed tickets to the event, which would be tastefully conducted inside the jail across the street from the capitol, out of view of those who didn't get official invites.

View from the capitol of the old Travis County Jail. The lockup is the castle-looking building in the upper right corner of the major intersection shown. *Author's collection.*

Austin had two competing dailies back then, the *Statesman* and the *Tribune*, a scrappy afternoon paper edited by Travis, then a young man of twenty-three. Travis had editorialized in favor of the man's hanging, an act he later came to regret. But he had not planned to cover the execution, preferring to leave that journalistic chore to one of his reporters. The *Tribune's* co-owner, however, wanted his best writer there. That would be Travis.

Travis, with a young reporter he took along just so he could show him the ropes (well, the rope), dutifully walked to the jail, a castle-looking stone structure behind the courthouse at 11th and Congress. Before the execution, the politically minded sheriff allowed Travis and the cub to talk with the condemned man in his cell.

"I told him there was a lot of talk that he could clear up several mysteries around town," Travis remembered. "He said that was true, but he wasn't going to do it. It would handicap his children, he said, and for their sake he was going to keep quiet. Well, that really touched me. And I told him so."

That, in turn, moved the barkeep.

"I'll clear up one for you," he said, confessing to a killing of which no one had suspected him.

Two men had been killed in a shootout in one of the saloons in the red-light district, and the bartender had been the only witness. Police concluded that each man had shot the other, but the barkeep told Travis that wasn't how it had been. One of the men had killed the other, but the bartender had risen from behind his bar and killed the first shooter.

Soon after his confession, the condemned man made his last walk.

As the barkeep faced his final moments, for Travis another sort of deadline loomed. He was running out of time to get the story in that afternoon's edition of the *Tribune*. The sheriff had thoughtfully set Travis up in an empty cell affording him a view of the metal gallows. The young editor sat at a small table, writing his story in longhand, sending out "takes" a page at a time to be rushed by messenger to the newspaper office seven blocks away. Travis had the middle and the ending of this story written, but he needed the beginning, the neck-breaking act that would be the barkeep's ending.

Meanwhile, back at the newspaper, part-owner Glen Pricer started getting nervous. The hanging was running late, but a p.m. paper couldn't wait forever on a story, even a big one. "He decided to come to the courthouse to see what was holding me up," Travis said. "About the time he got near the jail the condemned man came to the end of the rope, and it made a crack you could hear outside. Pricer fainted and fell down."

While helpful citizens carried the unconscious publisher into the courthouse, Travis scribbled away on his story. The barkeep had a black hood over his head, but the killing jerk when the rope went taut had nearly severed his head. It was not a pleasant scene. Travis wrote until he had said all he needed to say, and it all got in that day's edition.

He covered two more local legal hangings before the state switched to electrocution. "I was invited to forty-five executions down there [in Huntsville], but I never went to one," he said.

Matters of the Heart

Nice Love Letter from a Bad Man

Anyone familiar with state government knows that the legislature requires the various agencies and commissions to submit a biennial report. Most agencies, eager to show taxpayers and legislative budget writers their worth, not only gladly abide by this statute, but they prepare an annual report. Full of statistics and charts, most of these reports are not the sort of document a normal person would want to curl up with in front of a fireplace.

Not so the Adjutant General's Report for 1878, submitted by General William Steele to his Excellency, Governor R.B. Hubbard, on December 2 of that year. It has real content. At that time and for a good while thereafter, the Texas Rangers were a component of the Adjutant General's Department. From the El Paso Salt War to the violent demise of outlaw Sam Bass, 1878 had been an eventful year for the Rangers. All of which makes for interesting reading in this report. But there's more.

To illustrate the effectiveness of the Rangers in ridding the state of undesirables, General Steele included a letter "from a desperado…evidently a fugitive from justice in Texas, addressed to a woman here in Texas." Unfortunately for posterity, to protect the innocent, Steele did not include the name of the correspondent or the addressee. For that matter, the general also omitted just how the missive came into state hands. Even so, it is one of the most remarkable letters ever penned by a Texas outlaw, a class not generally known for literacy.

The bad guy, clearly a transplant to the Lone Star State, wrote the letter on September 1, 1878, from his camp in Dark Canyon, "Warloupe" Mountains, New Mexico. Known to accurate spellers as the Guadalupe Mountains, this range bridges Texas and New Mexico about one hundred miles east of El Paso.

Proudly, the outlaw told his belle he had traveled five hundred miles since his last letter. "This is headquarters for my gang," he said of aptly named Dark Canyon. "I have ten men with me—the best armed and best mounted outfit you ever saw. There are a war going on here between two strong parties [the Lincoln County, New Mexico war of Billy the Kid fame], and we have got an independent scout of our own. We just got in off of a raid, and made it pay us big."

While offering no further details, the gang leader seemed more worried about his girl than getting caught either by a lawman or a bullet. "Darling," he sweet-talked, "I am making money fast; but I see a hard time and am troubled to death about you. If I had you here I would be the happiest man on earth."

Alas, the girl of his dreams lived in Texas.

"This is the best country I ever saw," the outlaw continued, "and the healthiest country on earth."

Of course, good climate seldom could cure instant-onset lead poisoning. The knave continued: "On the twentieth day of August Gross and McGuire got into a fight, and McGuire shot him just below the heart, and I killed McGuire. I shot him through the heart. He never spoke after I shot him. We buried him as nice as we could, and sent Gross into the settlements, where he is being well treated. I think he will recover."

The outlaw may have just drilled someone through the heart, but his own heart had been stolen by his darling in Texas. "Oh, how I wish you were here," the self-confessed felon went on, "you would look like a child in six months. [Bold talk, even for an outlaw. Suggesting that something will make a woman look younger implies that she appears older than she is.] This is the finest watered country on earth, and the best climate; cool nights all summer."

That reminded the lover boy that he had gotten his girl a Navajo blanket, worth seventy-five dollars, "the prettiest thing you ever saw."

Well, that was about all the fellow knew or could tell. He closed, "Baby, take care of yourself, and be sure to write." Above his signature, he wrote, "From your loving one." All Steele included were the swain's initials, S.Z.

Who knows who S.Z. was and what happened to him or his ladylove? Since he had been plying the risky trade of outlawry, the best guess would be that he soon ended up on a cooling board preparatory to a Boot Hill burying.

But maybe not. Perhaps he and Miss Noname got married and she made an honest man of him. Or it could have worked the other way, him making a bad woman out of her.

Happily ever after, of course, usually only happens in fairy tales. Perhaps, if they did get together, they ended up splitting the sheets. But it's a good guess she kept the Navajo blanket.

A DOE AND A BRIDE

Anyone accidentally walking up on the young couple sitting on a wagon tongue near Brushy Creek outside Round Rock that day would have realized they were discussing something very important. Indeed, their topic had to do with the rest of their lives.

Twenty-seven-year-old Dick Tisdale—Kentucky-born, Round Rock–raised—had been up the Chisholm Trail and cowboyed in Montana and Idaho as well. Though they grew up only a few miles apart, he had not known eighteen-year-old Ada Saunders for very long. Dick quickly decided Ada was the girl he wanted to marry, but not quite yet. He thought he should make a little more money first. Quite smitten with the older, confident Tisdale, Ada agreed to wait for him, and she did.

Two years later, in the fall of 1886, Tisdale showed up in Round Rock with a rock of his own—a diamond engagement ring. Ada accepted it, but back then, a girl's father had to say yes, too. Tisdale went to see E.L. Saunders and asked for his daughter's hand in marriage. Not wanting to make a snap decision on something as important as his daughter's future, Saunders answered with no answer. Instead, he invited his daughter's suitor to join him on a deer hunt.

Though Williamson County had plenty of open country back then, the white-tail deer population had been hunted heavily for years with no thought toward conservation. The older farmer and the young cowboy hunted hard all day along a creek on Saunders's property but saw no game. Near sundown, they finally jumped a doe, which ran briefly before freezing in a stand of trees. "If you can get that deer, you can have her," Saunders told Tisdale.

Toting a shotgun loaded with buckshot, Tisdale raised the weapon, aimed at the doe and pulled the trigger. Mortally wounded, the doe ran a few yards on instinct and adrenaline before dropping dead.

At that, Saunders turned to face Tisdale. "You can have the girl," he told his future son-in-law. The two men field dressed the deer and went to see Ada. The family would have venison for supper and wedding plans to discuss.

A century later, two of their descendants—Marie C. Tisdale and Albert A. Tisdale—would tell the story of how Dick and Ada came to be married in a self-published family history, *Texas Cousins: Correll, Tisdale, and Related Families*. Nortex Press printed the book in 1986.

Getting back to Dick and Ada, on November 11, 1886, the couple exchanged their wedding vows at her home in Saunders, then a rail stop seven miles north of downtown Austin. They lived on the Saunders family farm between the small community named for the Saunders family and Round Rock. Dick made a living buying and selling mules.

After the birth of their first child in 1888, they moved to Georgetown, where Dick fed and sold cattle. In 1891, they had a second child. The couple stayed in Georgetown for more than a decade. In 1901, having made a little money in livestock, Dick bought four sections in Hartley County near Channing in the Panhandle. They relocated to the upper edge of the state, alternately making some money and surviving vicious, stock-killing winter weather or soil-baking droughts. In 1906, they sold their ranch, moved back to Central Texas and settled where they had started out, on the Saunders place not far from where some good shooting led to what must have been a good marriage.

The couple had another child when Ada was forty and went on to celebrate their golden wedding anniversary in 1936. Not long after that, Ada died, but Dick lived until January 1953, dying at age ninety-six.

The story of how a successful deer hunt made their marriage possible lives on in the family lore of their descendants.

CRITTERS

A ROOSTER GAVE HIS ALL FOR TEXAS

When news of the Alamo's fall reached Gonzales, it triggered panic among the Anglo population of Texas. Sam Houston ordered the town torched in advance of the Mexican army, and the residents fled for their lives to the east. Along the way, virtually every other settler joined the flight as Texas began to unravel in that late winter of 1836.

Elizabeth Zumwalt Kent, whose husband, Andrew Jackson Kent, had died in the Alamo, left the Gonzales area on foot with their ten children. Suffering in a climate that ranged from unseasonably cold to unseasonably wet, ten-year-old Elizabeth and her sixteen-month-old sister, Phinette, died of exposure. Andrew Kent, not yet four, became separated from his family during a stream crossing and was never seen again.

While not an exodus of biblical proportions, what came to be called the Runaway Scrape has not received the scholarly attention it deserves. Thousands of people hastily left their homes and most of their belongings hoping to outrun General Antonio Lopez de Santa Anna and his troops as he pushed into the heart of settled Texas following the massacre at the old mission in Bexar.

"A few days before we arrived in Gonzales," Mexican army Lieutenant Jose de la Pena wrote in his diary, "Generals Ramirez y Sesman and Tolsa had passed by, and the troops under their command had consumed and taken with them everything they could."

Courtesy Roger T. Moore.

By March 17, Washington-on-the-Brazos had been deserted. Within two weeks, all of Texas between the Colorado and Brazos Rivers lay virtually depopulated. Left behind were many fresh graves, including two for the Kent children.

The mass withdrawal continued until word spread of Houston's April 21 defeat of Santa Anna at San Jacinto. Slowly, those who still wanted to give life in Texas a chance, including Mrs. Kent, turned to the west and went back to what was left of their homes. And that's when a nameless hero would give his all for Texas.

"Our folks with their neighbors returned to their log houses on the south bank of the Colorado River," Smithville pioneer Rosa Berry Cole recalled in *Memories of By-Gone Days*. "Some found their houses burned, their crops gone and desolation everywhere, but they were free."

Their fences down and most of the rails burned, settlers had to start from scratch. Mrs. Kent discovered that the Mexicans had burned their cabin and slaughtered all their cattle, hogs and chickens. The blood and chop marks on Andrew's carpentry table showed it had been used as a butcher block.

Now, on top of everything else, the returning refugees faced a severe shortage of food and the means to produce it. Men saddled up to look for strayed milk cows while the womenfolk looked for loose chickens. Mrs. Cole managed to find three hens that had escaped the skillets of the Mexican army, and others living on or near the Colorado in Bastrop County found a few more.

But no one could find a rooster. No rooster, no chicks. No chicks, pretty soon no more setting hens or Sunday fried chicken dinners. Finally, someone heard that someone had a rooster for sale upriver in Bastrop. Neighbors passed a hat to raise enough money to buy the needed male of the species, and a volunteer rode to make the purchase.

The community rooster may not have fully appreciated his importance in rebuilding Texas, but he enthusiastically embraced the task at hand—and every hen along the river. As Cole recalled, people took the busy bird "from house to house, each keeping him a week till he made all the rounds and then back home and start over the same round." Before long, thanks to the seemingly undaunted patriotism of that rooster, Bastrop County residents never wanted for eggs or fried chicken.

Whether the rooster died of old age or exhaustion from loving too much isn't known, but his legacy kept clucking for a long time along the Colorado.

THE OLD REBEL BET ON A DEAD HORSE

Thomas Evans Riddle bet on a dead racehorse. The horse was Man o' War. Foaled in 1917, he won his first race, the Belmont Stakes, in 1919. He never took the Triple Crown, but in his short turf career, Man o' War came in first in twenty-five of his twenty-six races. Though owner Samuel D. Riddle lived in Pennsylvania, he usually kept Man o' War stabled in Kentucky. Still, both states claimed the wonder horse of the twentieth century. By the time he died at the age of thirty in 1947, the legendary racehorse had made his owner a millionaire several times over in stud fees.

Sam Riddle didn't live much longer after Man o' War died—about four years. When Sam died, he left his fortune to endow a hospital near his home in Philadelphia. That's when a new player entered the field, among others.

Thomas Riddle, then a 106-year-old Confederate veteran living in Texas, laid claim to a portion of Sam Riddle's estimated $4 million estate. In his deposition, Thomas attested that he was the late Sam's elder half brother. His attorney, Rodes K. Myers of Bowling Green, Kentucky, wanted his client to fly to Philadelphia for a court hearing with twenty-one others claiming to be legitimate Riddle heirs, but the old soldier's doctors refused to give him permission.

While the case languished in the courts of Philadelphia, Tom continued his daily games of checkers and dominoes with visitors. The last Civil War veteran living in the Confederate Home for Men at 1620 West Sixth Street in Austin, Tom had lots of visitors. And once the news got out that he might be an heir to a fortune, he had a lot of proposals of marriage from younger women.

Born on April 16, 1845, in Tennessee, Tom had served in the Twelfth Tennessee Infantry. He claimed that he spent eighteen months of his military time under General Robert E. Lee. The way Tom remembered it, General Lee himself chose Tom to care for the general's horse, Traveler. Tom said he fought with Lee at the Battle of Gettysburg in June and July 1863, sustaining a slight wound. But as he told the story, only thirteen men died in the pivotal battle, which of course was absolutely false. "I was there and we buried every one of them right there on the field," he said. He didn't remember the battle as a big deal.

Man o' War is considered one of the great racehorses of all time. *Author's collection.*

Tom came to Texas in 1879 from Tennessee, settling in Grayson County, where, for twenty-three years, he made a living as a stonemason and farmer. But after several discouraging years of drought, boll weevils and grasshoppers, he packed up his wife and kids and moved westward to Clay County.

Later, Tom lived in Wichita Falls before moving to the Confederate Home in January 1950. When he first arrived, he enjoyed taking frequent walks around the twenty-six-acre campus overlooking the Colorado River, but his advanced age soon caught up with him.

The home was built in 1884 by a volunteer group of former members of General John Bell Hood's Texas Brigade at a cost of $500,000. Eight years later, the State of Texas took control of the facility. Over time, the rambling frame building with wide steps and a tall tower accommodated 3,800 veterans. By 1943, only 6 former soldiers remained, and the home began admitting aged male patients from other hospitals.

At the Confederate Home, Riddle kept a portrait of Lee and a Confederate battle flag near his bed. He never earned rank in Lee's Army of Virginia, but the State of Texas and others heaped honorary titles on him, including colonel of the Confederate Air Force.

The old soldier had a television set in his room and liked to keep up with the news of the Korean War. He may have watched films of Pork Chop Hill in April 1953. The same month, the home's staff, members of the Austin Chapter of the Daughters of the Confederacy and local residents helped Riddle celebrate his 106th birthday.

Tom lived just one more year. After bouts with pneumonia and heart failure, the old soldier died on April 2, 1954, two weeks shy of his 107th birthday. Four days later, he was buried in North Texas at Burkburnett.

In 1956, the Riddle fortune went to support the hospital in Pennsylvania, as Sam Riddle had intended. No matter whether he truly had a blood tie to the man who had owned Man o' War, death had dropped Tom Riddle from the run for the money.

OLE MAGGIE

Maggie—folks called her Mag—was some gal. They said she was the first of her kind born in Lampasas County. While that might be hard to substantiate, she went on to become not only a local celebrity but nationally known as well. Though she hailed from around Bend, a Colorado River community in San Saba County, and spent a good half of her life in Lampasas County, she earned her reputation one day in Goldthwaite in neighboring Mills County.

Of Mag's genealogy, no record is known to exist. But to Cornelius McAnelly, who worked with her when she was young, Mag was like family. He took care of her when she was old, blind and hard of hearing, even though he had to see to it from his wheelchair. None of what McAnelly did was any different from what just about anyone would do for kith or kin. But caring so strongly for a female like Mag was a little unusual, considering Mag was a mule.

Born in 1891, Mag did not seem any different from any other mule. But she could pull a "Georgia stock" mold-board plow all day long in the blazing sun and make it look easy. She worked hard, learned fast and ran faster.

That's how she came to clean the pockets of numerous Mills County residents one day during her prime. Someone, maybe McAnelly, perhaps a sporting friend, took bets that Mag could outrun any pony in the county. The improbability of a mule outrunning a pony proved to be an irresistible bet. After everyone had their money down and the starting handkerchief dropped, as one writer later put it, "The pony was almost suffocated by mule dust." And $300, back when that was as much cash as some folks earned in a year of hard work, changed hands as a result.

Mag was so fast she got into the rodeo world as a roping animal. As the years went by, it became increasingly evident that a strong life force coursed through her veins. But by her late teens, time had begun to catch up with Mag and her owner. McAnelly, born in 1856, was the first Anglo child born in Lampasas County. Mag was the oldest mule in Lampasas County.

About 1919, McAnelly and others began to realize that Mag not only was past her prime but by all rights she ought to be dead. Yet she lived on. True, she was too old to work, but the McAnellys had pretty much quit farming anyway. "Uncle Neil" and his wife held onto their land along the Colorado but moved to Lometa, in Mills County. Mag went with them, as much a member of their family as their children and grandchildren.

McAnelly kept his pet mule tied up under the shade trees in his yard, seeing to it that she got bran, oats or cottonseed meal three times a day. Though long in the tooth, there wasn't anything wrong with her chomping ability. She could make ten ears of corn look smooth as rolling pins in a matter of moments.

As word spread that a mule born in 1891 was still kicking—figuratively and literally—as the Jazz Age turned into a worldwide financial depression, folks started coming around to see Old Mag. Reporters strapped for hard news stories took to interviewing Mag, coming up with some pretty erudite quotes considering they were articulated by a mule. Judging from the remarks attributed to her, she could give Will Rogers a run for his money in the wise and witty category. In short, Mag's long life made her a media star.

One of her last interviews was in 1934 with Sam Ashburn, longtime agricultural writer for the *San Angelo Standard-Times*. How much longer after that she kept eating corn and offering the wisdom that can only come from someone who has seen a lot of summers is not known, but "Uncle Neil" McAnelly died on November 24, 1935. His wife made it for nearly another decade.

Who knows? Maybe whoever it was in Hollywood who came up with the idea of a television show called *Francis the Talking Mule* had read about Mag the talking mule—an old lady with a reputation in three counties.

CHARACTERS

MARK WITHERS

Back in Texas's trail-driving days, a cow pony could cause a man an awful lot of worry—especially a horse with idiosyncrasies.

One day in the 1870s, Mississippi-born Mark Withers left his Caldwell County ranch to gather another herd of cattle to drive to market in Kansas. Years later, he told the story of what happened next to his son-in-law, the late Holland Page of Lockhart.

In Bastrop to buy some stock, Withers saw a horse that caught his fancy. He purchased the pony, too, to ride up the trail. A wise cattleman didn't just take one horse on a long journey, no matter what Western movies would have people believe. He took several mounts so as not to ride one pony to death. Even so, a cowboy generally developed a liking for a certain horse. In Withers's case, he became particularly fond of the pony he'd bought in Bastrop.

The only hitch with the animal was that it wouldn't stand being hitched. But the solution was simple enough. If a rider dropped the pony's reins to the ground, the horse would stay put on its own. The Bastrop man warned Withers that tying the horse to something would lead to trouble.

Withers soon realized he had made a wise choice in buying the pony, despite its aversion to being tied. The cattle drive went well, too, Withers making good money in marketing his beeves at the railhead. The economic chaos of the Civil War still fresh on his mind, the Texas stockman preferred to sell his steers for gold instead of paper money. Sometimes, however, he had to settle for a combination of both. That proved to be the case on this particular drive, and Withers headed back to Texas with a saddlebag full of gold and cash astride the rump of the horse he'd bought in Bastrop.

Somewhere in Indian Territory one day, Withers got hungry and galloped to the chuck wagon for some grub. His appetite must have dulled his memory, because he forgot and tied up the horse that didn't like being tied. The first time the famished Withers looked up from his tin plate, he realized his horse had vanished—and with it many thousands of dollars. His appetite having disappeared along with his fortune, Withers quickly saddled another horse from his remuda and tried to find the tracks of the richest horse on either side of the Red River.

For two weeks, Withers and his cowhands hunted the four-footed treasure in the thick brush along that portion of the cattle trail. Finally, worn out, broke and still owing money he had borrowed to buy the cattle, Withers dejectedly turned south for home on one of his less eccentric horses. Back in Central Texas, he sadly explained to his wife that they faced big trouble. His carelessness had cost them their future, not to mention a good horse.

A few weeks later, still devastated over the loss of his hard-earned money, Withers received a penny postcard from the man who had sold him the cattle and the now-missing horse. The peregrinating pony, still carrying its saddle and saddlebags, had shown up in Bastrop—more than three hundred miles from where Withers had last seen it.

In the old West, the arrival of a rider-less horse usually portended bad news. Could be, the former owner logically figured, Withers lay dead somewhere, killed by Indians, crushed in a stampede or drowned crossing a river. It could have been any number of things. Even so, the Bastrop man had sent the stray notice to Withers's address in Lockhart. Until he learned for sure what had become of Withers, he put the horse out to pasture and stored Withers's gear in his barn.

After reading the card, Withers constituted a one-man stampede getting to Bastrop from Lockhart. The seller took Withers to his barn, where the cattleman ripped open his saddlebags like a kid tearing the wrapping from his only birthday present. His gold and greenbacks had not been touched. Thanking the Bastrop man for his integrity, Withers led his favorite horse and the proceeds from his long, hard trail drive back to Caldwell County.

A few years before he died in 1938, the old cattleman told his son-in-law that the close call he had with the picky pony stood as one of the greatest experiences of his long life. Withers had kept the horse for many years, but he darn sure never tied it up again.

LIEUTENANT WILL PORTER

The mustachioed young man from North Carolina hardly seemed the martial type, but as a citizen soldier in the Austin Grays, he demonstrated the qualities of a leader—even if he used those management skills to keep from spending the night in the guardhouse.

In the early summer of 1886, he and his fellow guardsmen boarded the train for Lampasas, a city seventy miles northwest of Austin then touted as the "Saratoga of the South."

Since the arrival of the first settlers in the 1850s, the springs along the well-named Sulfur Creek had been thought to have medicinal qualities. When the Santa Fe Railroad reached Lampasas in 1882, developers sought to transform the town into a resort. Construction soon started on a grand hotel and bathhouse. For a time the largest frame-built hostelry in the state, the two-story Park Hotel looked like a giant mansion. Wide galleries lined each floor of the 331-foot-long structure, which had two hundred guest rooms, hot and cold bathing pools, dressing rooms, concession facilities and a ballroom large enough to seat a full orchestra.

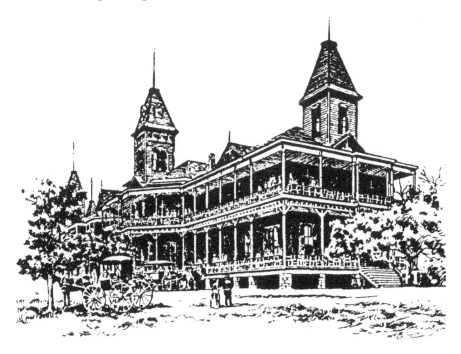

Porter and his fellow Austin Grays partied at the ornate Park Hotel at Lampasas. *Author's collection.*

But the volunteers arriving at the Lampasas depot had not come to town to take the waters. They had gathered to sharpen their military skills at the annual encampment of the Texas Volunteer Guard, the predecessor of today's National Guard.

Though the Austin Grays stood ready to defend their state, the company was more social group than fighting outfit. And few Austinites could be considered more convivial than Lieutenant Will Porter, a southern gentleman known for his bass singing voice, his sense of humor and his taste for beer. In addition to their membership in the Grays, Porter and three other guardsmen made up the Hill City Quartette, a well-known

Will Porter, better known as O. Henry, could think on his feet. *Author's collection.*

singing group. The quartet received permission to go on leave one night to perform at a grand ball at the equally grand Park Hotel. Between sets, the sharply uniformed Austin boys had no trouble finding attractive, interested dance partners. Tripping the light fantastic and perhaps enjoying too many cups of champagne punch, the quartet lost track of time.

About five minutes after they were supposed to be back in camp, someone finally noticed the hour. By then, the officer of the day at the nearby military tent city already had a squad en route to the hotel to arrest the tardy guardsmen.

Thinking fast, Porter got a friend to meet the squad at the door and suggest that since there were ladies present, the soldiers should stack their rifles outside before entering. The corporal in charge agreed that it would not be proper to make the belles at the ball uncomfortable and ordered his men to put down their weapons. As the soldiers walked into the hotel, Porter and several of his comrades slipped out a side door and retrieved their artillery. Porter then herded all the unarmed AWOL guardsmen into formation and briskly marched them back to camp as if he had them under arrest.

"None of us knew the countersign, and our success in getting by the sentry was a matter of pure grit," one of the participants later recalled. "As we approached…we were crossing a narrow plank bridge in single file, at the end of which the sentry threw up his gun and Porter marched us right straight up to that gun until the front man was marking time with the point of the gun right at his stomach." Staring down the sentry, Porter barked: "Squad under arrest. Stand aside!"

Once inside the camp, the imposters stacked their arms and quietly disappeared into their tents. A short time later, the embarrassed corporal of the guard and his unarmed men returned without their prisoners. The sentry did not buy his story and had the whole squad marched to the guardhouse.

"There was quite a time at the [corporal's] court-martial next morning," Porter's old guard buddy wrote, "but no one ever knew our connection to the story."

One of Porter's biographers speculated that the tale might have been embellished a bit, but the man who told it declared: "This adventure is only one of thousands of such incidents that commonly occurred in his life."

Porter, under the pen name of O. Henry, went on to make a career out of adventure. His worldwide fame has endured, though the incident at Lampasas is as long forgotten as the old Park Hotel, destroyed by fire in 1895.

BILL WHARTON

Used to be, especially in the eighteenth and nineteenth centuries, some people were born Thankful and died Thankful. That's because, way back, parents sometimes named their daughters Thankful.

Born in 1803, Thankful Rankin later married someone with a more common given name, William Watson Wharton. Well into middle age, the couple made their way to the Texas Hill Country in 1857. Thankful and her husband relocated from McNary County in Tennessee to Kerr County. They bought 640 acres along the old Guadalupe River road between Kerrville and Center Point, a route that came to be called Wharton Road.

William and Thankful gave thanks for their new home and for their three sons, one of whom was William G. Wharton, born in 1841. Folks called him Bill. Just shy of his twenty-first birthday when the Civil War broke out, Bill served as a sergeant in Company A of the Mounted Regiment of Texas State Troops, a unit that functioned as Rangers to protect the frontier from hostile Indians. Whenever he heard the word "thankful," Wharton thought of his mother, but her sainted name also summarized his position on chewing

Bill Wharton rode as a Texas Ranger and later raised cattle. *Author's collection.*

tobacco, hound dogs, whiskey and his six-shooter. He had high gratitude for all those things. Following his discharge from Confederate duty, Bill returned to Kerr County to raise cattle and occasionally serve as a peace officer.

His father died in 1871, occupying one of the earliest graves in the Wharton Family Cemetery, founded the year before. Thankful lived another fifteen years before joining her husband in the small graveyard.

At some point, Bill Wharton's long, interesting life moved someone to poetry. Panhandle artist H.D. Bugbee published the untitled poem in 1960, not saying who had written it. Wharton family descendants believe it was the work of Anne L. Black, a niece of Bill's wife, Lucia, who most members of the family knew as Aunt Lou. Aunt Anne, as her younger relatives called her, was a poet who published a collection of her work late in life. While the poem about Bill is not in the book, the family says its style matches Black's known work. But the book does have a poem titled "Aunt Lou," set in Kerrville, so the family's probably right in deducing that Black is the author.

No matter who wrote it, Bugbee featured the poem along with a pen-and-ink sketch of Wharton in a small booklet printed by Clarendon Press, "Bill Wharton or an Example of Early Hill Country Diplomacy." Today, the small piece about Wharton, his propensity to go around heeled and an understanding county sheriff is quite collectible and quite scarce.

Though no mention is made in the poem of the Second Amendment and the right to keep and bear arms it guarantees, old Bill seems to have been one of those types who didn't feel properly dressed without a pistol hanging on his side. No subtlety in its rhyme, here's the poem:

> *Bill Wharton was a cowman in an early Kerrville day;*
> *He also was a lawman—in a carefree sort of way.*
>
> *His ranch was on the Rock Springs road, he lived there with Aunt Lou.*
> *It made an ideal stopping place for travelers passing through.*
>
> *For as long as they would visit he encouraged them to stay;*
> *A sittin', spittin' on the porch, the true Bill Wharton way.*
>
> *Wherever that old man would go, his hound dogs went there too.*
> *There wasn't anything, he said, "them hound dogs couldn't do."*
>
> *Quite often into Kerrville he'd come and bring his wife—*
> *For he loved the Kerrville liquor and the Kerrville brand of life.*
>
> *Then they passed a law in Texas, guns must not be worn in view,*
> *So deputizing Wharton was the only thing to do.*

It wasn't aught that he had sought, that badge pinned on his vest,
'Twas kind of forced upon him with the taming of the West.

Since boyhood every morning he had donned his pants and gun;
They couldn't make him give 'em up, no sir, either one.

He wouldn't have felt decent without his gun and belt,
It was lucky that the sheriff realized that was how Bill felt.

For fifty years he wore that gun, no doubt he packs it still—
For if he didn't folks would say, "that cain't be Uncle Bill."

Bill Wharton died on November 3, 1919, and lies buried with his kinfolk in the family cemetery. Whether he was still packing a shooting iron when they lowered him into his grave is another unanswered question. If so, he doubtless would have invoked his mother's name for the eternal protection.

MELCHER'S EXTERMINATOR

The stinging fire ant would not invade Texas for another century, but the Lone Star State had no shortage of pesky critters in the 1870s. Back then, folks who made their living in agricultural pursuits considered cutter ants and the "California ground squirrel, commonly known as the gopher," particularly onerous. The gopher, declared German immigrant J.C. Melcher, "is a great pest to the farmer, destroying quantities of grain and doing great injury to gardens and orchards."

Melcher and his wife had come to Texas by way of Galveston. En route to the German settlement of New Braunfels, they found the Colorado River flooded. While they waited for the water to go down, Melcher had ample time to visit with ferry owner and Fayette County pioneer John Moore, also a noted Indian fighter. When Moore found out that Melcher was a cabinetmaker, he said that a man proficient at that trade could make a good living right there. Moore soon convinced Melcher to forget about New Braunfels and stay in Fayette County.

In 1855, Melcher decided he could do better as a retailer than a cabinetmaker and opened a general store at Black Jack Springs, a community between La Grange and Flatonia. While meeting the retail needs of his customers, he heard plenty of sad stories about crop-eating critters.

A creative sort who, despite his success as a merchant, still liked to make things with his hands, Melcher invented a solution. He called it "The Victory Ant, Mole, Gopher and Ground Squirrel Exterminator." The Exterminator consisted of two major components, a cast-iron "fire chamber" and a wooden pump. The operator heated sulfur with coal in the twelve- by twenty-four-inch furnace, causing a buildup of sulfurous gas in the chamber. The device had a sharpened flange that went into the ground over a gopher or ant hole. The eleven- by eleven-inch pump, nearly three feet high, at thirty strokes a minute pushed two cubic feet of gas into a pest's underground domicile. That much gas, Melcher asserted, could fill a two-inch gopher hole two thousand feet long with deadly fumes.

The Fayette County man's invention must have been quite effective. His Exterminator won first place at the 1879 State Fair of Texas, an event then held in Austin. Melcher received an ornate "Diploma," complete with an engraving of the limestone capitol that would burn down a few years later.

Less than a month after winning his prize, on November 18, 1879, Melcher received from the U.S. Patent Office a patent for his pest-control device.

Word of the invention's effectiveness soon spread. The January 3, 1880 edition of *Scientific American* had a story on the Exterminator that gave it and its creator national recognition.

Melcher soon went to a job printer and had a handbill run off. "I have manufactured over four hundred pumps during the last few years," the inventor-entrepreneur said in the advertising piece, "and have taken great pains to bring them as near perfection as possible and will continue to improve them if I possibly can."

The piece also announced that "territorial rights" to sell the device could be purchased "very cheap for cash, land, notes, or other good property." Just how many salesmen Melcher recruited and how well his business went is not known by his descendants.

Melcher stayed in Fayette County, but in the early 1900s, one of his sons, Edmund Max Melcher, decided to seek new opportunities elsewhere in the state. Narrowing his options down to either Houston or the growing port city of Port Lavaca, Melcher flipped a coin. Port Lavaca won the toss, and his branch of the family has been in Calhoun County ever since.

After settling in the coastal town, he worked as a clerk at the Bay City Trading Company for several years. In 1912, he and a partner opened a general merchandise store. Five years later, Melcher purchased a building at 203 East Main Street and opened a hardware store. The place has been in business ever since. Ed Melcher's son, J.C. Melcher II, inherited the store and kept it open through the Depression and assorted hurricanes. Today, J.C. Melcher III, great-grandson of the inventor of the Exterminator, still runs the family hardware store. Hanging on the wall in a room filled with old merchandise is a copy of the handbill J.C. Melcher printed to advertise his invention.

Unfortunately, that piece of paper is the only known evidence of Melcher's product. A fire at the old family homestead at Black Jack Springs destroyed Melcher's house and any unsold Exterminators he might have had around.

TEXAS'S TWO-LEGGED HOGG

His second term in office nearly complete, the governor gave a speech in Rockdale, reflecting both on his accomplishments and his state of mind. James Stephen Hogg, the first native-born Texas governor, had moved from typesetting to newspaper editing to practicing law. His first elected office was as a justice of the peace in the East Texas town of Quitman. By 1886, he was attorney general, and in 1890, he was elected governor.

The only setback in Hogg's political ascendency came in a loss for a legislative seat in 1876, but he paid for his smooth-sailing career during the election campaign of 1892–93. In a state still known for contentious politics, that campaign, familiar these days only to students of Texas political history, still stands out.

Running against Hogg in his quest for a second term was Judge George Clark of Waco. Like Hogg, he was a lawyer, but unlike Hogg, who weighed 350 pounds, Clark was of small stature. But he was a political king maker whose friends called him the Little Giant.

Back then, Texas for all practical purposes was a one-party state. The two Democratic factions, however, acted like separate parties. Hogg was portrayed as the protector of the common man. Clark was seen as the lackey of the corporate big boys. "Control the corporations" was Hogg's slogan. "Turn Texas loose," countered the Clark camp.

Political wars of this era were waged on the pages of newspapers, in handbills and in public appearances and rallies. Long before anyone conceived television attack ads, political attacks were as likely to be physical as rhetorical. The Clark-Hogg campaign touched off numerous fistfights in

Governor James Stephen Hogg. *Courtesy Texas State Archives.*

communities across the state. "Brother was often arrayed against brother and father against son," Judge C.V. Terrell later recalled. "The closest ties of friendship were too often severed."

A couple of campaign debates ended so raucously that both sides, fearing serious violence, wisely agreed to schedule no more. The party's state convention, held in Houston, threatened to get entirely out of hand. When Hogg's supporters set up boxes to prevent Clark delegates from reaching the elevated platform at the head of the makeshift convention hall, the pro-Clark forces vacated the premises and set up their own meeting at city hall.

The gathering concluded without any injuries or deaths, but on election day, the state had two full Democratic slates to pick from. Despite the support of most of the bigger city daily newspapers, Clark and his fellow candidates did not prevail in the popular vote. The man called Texas's only two-footed hog won reelection by nearly 200,000 votes.

Looking back on his service to the state in that speech at Rockdale, Hogg listed what he considered his successes. The primary one was pushing through the creation of the Railroad Commission (originally intended to regulate the railroad industry; only later did it get oversight of the oil industry).

"Let us have Texas, the Empire State, governed by the people," the governor later said, "not Texas, the truck-patch, ruled by corporate lobbyists."

The law creating the Railroad Commission was one of five bills he signed into law that gave the state more control over big corporations. Hogg also championed the need for an open records law, but that would not come until much later.

"For once in my life," Hogg said in his Rockdale speech, "I am at peace with the world and mankind, politically, personally and socially. This condition sheds with much force the light of happiness upon my heart."

The governor had a similar hope for his native state. What he wished was that "never again shall political storms, from necessity or otherwise, rise to disturb the equilibrium, repose, tranquility and good order of our people."

Hogg has been at peace since his death on March 3, 1906. The political storms, however, continue to rise.

LANDMARKS

WACO'S COTTON PALACE

The State Fair is a Texas institution, but during the first three decades of the twentieth century, hundreds of thousands of people headed to big doings in Waco each fall, not Dallas. Now practically forgotten, the Cotton Palace rivaled the State Fair and showcased Waco for the world up until 1930.

The wife of a Waco lawyer—a later history identifies her only as Mrs. Joe Taylor—may have been the first person to articulate the idea of an event in Central Texas highlighting the cotton industry. "Why not a Cotton Palace at Waco, the Queen City of the Brazos?" she asked in a Waco newspaper on January 23, 1890.

Mrs. Taylor and others had heard of a successful annual fair in Nebraska staged in a structure called the Corn Palace and thought the concept would work in Texas. Nebraska had plenty of corn, and Texas, especially Waco, had plenty of cotton. In fact, the city on the Brazos was the largest inland cotton market in Texas and one of the largest in the South. Some 120,000 bales of cotton were sold in the city in 1893.

It took the Cotton Palace idea little longer to germinate than a good cotton crop. With an organizational structure in place by 1894, plans were drawn for an exhibition hall in Waco's Padgett Park. The fair opened on November 8 that year and ran until December 6. Governor James Stephen Hogg attended the inaugural ceremonies, and thousands of visitors made the event a success.

As the caption on this early postcard declares, Waco's Cotton Palace was considered the South's "most unique exposition." *Author's collection.*

The 1894 fair might have been the beginning of a long run except for what happened on January 19, 1895: the ornate frame "palace" built the year before caught fire and burned down as "ten thousand Wacoans watched and wept."

Despite the success of the first fair, it took another fifteen years for the Cotton Palace to bloom again. This time, with a big new palace and numerous other buildings covering a twelve-acre site in Padgett Park, the fair took root.

Beginning in 1910, the fair ran for the next twenty-one years, becoming one of the most successful such events in the nation. Attendance grew with the extent of events. In 1912, former Waco mayor Robert Ross, an old Indian fighter and Civil War veteran, brought a delegation of Huaco Indians to the fair from Oklahoma. The Indians set up their tepees on the fairgrounds and performed dances on a regular schedule each day.

During World War I, with 10,000 soldiers stationed at Waco's Camp MacArthur, the military offered sham battles and biplane flyovers. When 117,208 people visited the fair on November 3, 1923, it set an all-time attendance record. And every year, the coronation of the Cotton King and Queen reigned as the city's premier social event.

The annual Cotton Palace festivities continued until 1930, when the Depression wilted the cotton market and most other aspects of the nation's economy. The fair closed on October 19 that year for the final time. An estimated eight million people had visited the fair during its twenty-one-year existence.

World War II revitalized the economy—Waco became the largest producer of military tents during the conflict—but the city's importance as a cotton center declined, and the Cotton Palace was history.

While the only tangible reminder of the fair in Waco is a monument in Cameron Park made from the cornerstone of the old palace, in 1970 a group of Wacoans produced a historical pageant called *The Waco Cotton Palace*. The annual two-hour show, staged in the spring, is still going strong.

SEBASTOPOL

The old town of Seguin has a secret only a handful of architectural historians and archaeologists know about.

Someone less inclined to honor the memory of Texas hero Erasmo Seguin could as easily have named the seat of Guadalupe County Concretetown. Or, more appropriately, Limecretetown.

Limecrete was an early form of concrete made of just the right mixture of lime, water and gravel. Nineteenth-century Seguin had as many as one hundred limecrete structures, more than any other city in Texas. Most of the houses are gone now, but one striking example remains: Sebastopol. Also known as the Zorn House, the Greek Revival–style home was built between 1854 and 1856 by Joshua Young. The process consisted of putting up wooden forms and then pouring in limecrete to make the foundation and walls. Actually, Young probably only supervised the construction. Slaves are believed to have done the real work.

The obvious question: why concrete? A construction material most people associate with the urban sprawl of the twentieth century, its use actually dates to Roman times. However, its use was not common in nineteenth-century Texas, except around Seguin, where some houses were built of limecrete as early as the 1840s. The answer to the concrete question is that while lumber for frame houses had to come by wagon from Indianola on the coast, gravel and limestone could be obtained in plentiful quantity right there in Guadalupe County. Too, ample timber stood along the Guadalupe River for use in building the forms for concrete walls. Finally, the community had no shortage of water.

Bricks also could be made locally—and were—but that was a more labor-intensive process. Also, using bricks in construction took a higher skill level than was generally available in the area at the time. But with ample raw material, slave labor and enough craftsmen who knew how to properly mix the necessary ingredients, building structures with concrete made plenty of sense. The concept of energy conservation had not been invented yet, but concrete houses obviously offered better insulation than frame structures, staying cooler in the summer and being easier to heat in the winter.

Young sold his concrete house to his sister in 1857, and it remained in her family until 1874, when Joseph Zorn Jr. purchased it. A businessman, Zorn served as Seguin's mayor from 1890 to 1910. He and his wife raised six children in the house, which stayed in his family's possession until 1961, when Zorn's granddaughter Hazel Tegener sold the house to the Seguin Conservation Society.

That group renovated the house and kept it open to the public until 1976, when the Texas Parks and Wildlife Department bought it and transformed it into the Sebastopol State Historical Park. Before stabilizing and restoring the old house, the state contracted for a thorough

Architecturally, Seguin's Sebastopol is one of the most interesting structures in Texas. *Courtesy Texas Parks and Wildlife Department.*

archaeological investigation of the structure. According to the report, archaeologists recovered more than 100,000 artifacts in excavating the floors and around the foundation of the house. The fifteen-foot-deep limecrete cistern near the house contained a huge cache of artifacts, from broken dishes to old medicine bottles. The most striking find was an object that tends to support the belief that slaves once worked and lived on the property: a rare black ceramic toy called a Charlie doll.

The site remained under state management until 2011, when the City of Seguin took over operation of the built-to-last old house.

COVERT PARK, AKA MOUNT BONNELL

Next time you're in Austin, be sure to visit Covert Park. But if you don't know how to get there, don't ask someone where it is. If you need directions, just ask how to find Mount Bonnell.

Most Austinites don't know that one of the prettiest places in their city is officially known as Covert Park. That's in honor of Frank M. Covert Sr., who in 1938 donated to Travis County a tract of land that back then lay just beyond the western edge of town. The centerpiece of the property was Mount Bonnell. In the early 1970s, the city acquired the land and turned it into Covert Park.

Mount Bonnell is generally accepted as having been named for pioneer Texan George M. Bonnell. Some argue, however, that the landmark was named after one Joseph Bonnell, a West Point graduate who served both in the U.S. military and later the Republic of Texas's army. Regardless of which Mr. Bonnell the prominence honors, it's not a mountain in the real sense of the word. But it is the highest point in Austin—some 775 to 785 feet above sea level and about 200 feet above the body of water just beneath it, Lake Austin.

Still, the view from the top is impressive. And people have been coming to enjoy that vista for a long time. In 1841, as the *Austin Daily Bulletin* reported on December 13, "A large party of ladies and gentlemen incited by the fineness of the weather and making use of the vacant time during the temporary adjournment of Congress made an excursion on Saturday morning to Mount Bonnell and the country adjacent." The newspaper editor, in recounting the excursion, noted that his "editorial duties" had "precluded [him] from the pleasure of participation."

But it seemed to him that just about everyone else in town made the trip. "The party consisted of 40 gentlemen and 10 ladies, who returned to town in formal array, the armed portion of the cavalcade in advance," the *Bulletin* account continued. Texas Vice President Edward Burleson had made the trip, along with the charge of a foreign nation (France), members of the republic's Congress, "professional men and plain citizens, many of them temporary visitants... who will certainly go home with a vivid recollection of the sunny and variegated beauty of the scenery around Austin and the salubrity of its atmosphere."

A historical marker at Mount Bonnell. *Photo by the author.*

The reason the excursionists had to have an armed escort was that Austin then constituted the farthest outpost of settlement on the Texas frontier. The Indians still had not accepted that Texas had declared itself a sovereign nation. Despite the threat of Indians, the editor of the *Bulletin* obviously hated that he had missed the trip. "We wanted to scent the pure air of the mountains," he waxed on, clearly needing some time out of the office, "to encircle with the heart's vision the beauty of the scene, to look again over the dark blue peaks of which the memory of our boyhood still has some reminisces, and upon the river with its gentle current running far beneath, and the wood upon its borders, for we think it one of the pleasantest sights in nature to look down upon running water and the varied verdance of a forest."

Those who did go, the editor continued, got the view and good groceries: "The viands which were carried out and partaken of by the Cypress spring in the valley, would to us have had an improved taste engendered by the pure air and the novelty and beauty of the scene."

All in all, the editor concluded, the excursion to Mount Bonnell had been "merry as a marriage bell." Still lamenting that he had missed the outing, the editor philosophized, "We count such a day's enjoyment, worth a year of common life, and reiterate our regret at not having been there."

Sam Houston, just beginning his second term as president of the republic, had not been there either, but he had visited Mount Bonnell. Houston once climbed the peak with Judge R.M. Williamson, a former Texas Ranger. The big general is supposed to have slapped Williamson on the back and proclaimed: "Upon my soul, Williamson, this must be the very spot where Satan took our Savior to show and tempt him with the riches and beauties of this world."

NAMELESS CAVE

It figures that the cave in this story—one of an estimated six thousand caverns in the limestone region of the state—doesn't have a name. After all, it's somewhere in the vicinity of Nameless, Texas. Located in northwest Travis County, once a half-day's horseback ride from a capitol staffed by anonymous bureaucrats who reported to various elected officials who generally hated to be nameless, the town with no name got used to being Nameless.

Bureaucracy, in fact, helped give Nameless its name. A decade after the first settlers put down roots in 1869, the citizens of this community felt they needed their own post office. Officials in Washington did not disagree, but they would not accept the name the townspeople proposed. Nor would the feds approve the second, the third, the fourth, the fifth or the sixth name submitted.

Finally, the story goes, someone involved in the civic effort to improve communication in their community said in disgust, "Let the post office be nameless and be damned." The Post Office Department had far too many decent people on its staff to approve the latter choice, but showing that government can be capable of humor, the post office finally received in 1880 its official designation: Nameless, Texas.

Four years later, Nameless boasted a school, a general store, a church and a population of fifty. That's about when a fellow named Barrett moved to Nameless from Illinois. Barrett may have been a Yankee trying to make a living in a barely reconstructed South, but folks had to give him one thing— he appreciated a good story.

About the best story Nameless had to offer other than how it got its name had to do with a hermit. The earliest residents of the town told of an old man who lived in a nearby cave, hording a treasure. Hearing the tale of the old geezer and his supposed treasure, Barrett determined to find it. As the *Austin Daily Statesman* reported on June 18, 1885, "Mr. Barrett with true Yankee ingenuity invented what he termed a 'mineral rod,' which he claims possesses the power of indicating to the operator the presence of 'filthy lucre' in mineral shape." The device had one catch: whoever held the rod could not carry any loose change.

"I will add just here," the unnamed Nameless correspondent wrote, "nine-tenths of our citizens are eminently qualified to successfully operate the 'mineral rod.'"

Though the treasure had been lost for no one knew how long, just about everyone in Nameless could name the location of the cave in question. With its opening on the side of a cliff about two hundred feet above Sandy Creek, it extended deep into the limestone. "Owing to the inaccessible situation and the ghost stories connected with it," the correspondent corresponded, "no one before Mr. B. ever had the temerity to explore it."

But on the morning of June 16, Barrett emptied his pockets and braved the cave. From the top of the cliff, he had someone lower him a basket containing his "mineral rod," a pick and other tools. Then he began his exploration. Barrett found a large cavern full of dripping stalactites, "which formed beautiful columns from floor to roof." That was nothing. "Situated in the centre of the room in an elevation something like a throne, sat the king of Goblins," the *Statesman* correspondent continued with what readers had to assume was a straight face, "our legendary, but now real, hermit."

Long petrified, the body's right hand rested "on the head of a small statue representing Louis Napoleon, and [in] his left, pressed to his heart, was a crucifix. At his feet lay the petrified remains of a dog, and scattered around the room, were remains of several things which doubtless once composed his furniture and utensils."

One thing, however, did not turn up in the underground wonderland: the treasure. At least not on Barrett's first visit. "The cave and its contents are of unusual interest, and Mr. B. does not wish to be interrupted until he has made a thorough exploration, after which he will satisfy the public," the newspaper writer concluded.

Apparently, the public never got satisfied. No further mention of the matter is made in subsequent editions of the Austin newspaper. If Barrett or anyone else ever discovered the hermit's treasure, he must have preferred to remain nameless.

BARTON SPRINGS

Many see Barton Springs, the fourth-largest natural waterworks in the state, as the soul of Austin. At first thought, that might seem a relatively modern viewpoint, but the cold, crystal clear waters emptying into the Colorado River have been attracting attention for a long time. Indians camped there centuries before Europeans arrived in what would become Texas, and the Spanish are believed to have built a temporary mission there, even though no traces of it have ever been found.

Possibly the earliest international attention given Barton Springs came in the 1840s, back when "America" meant three things to geography-minded Britons: Canada, the United States and Texas. British publications reflected an ongoing interest with developments in the former colonies and the upstart nation called the Republic of Texas.

In Scotland, brothers William and Robert Chambers published the *Edinburgh Journal*, a weekly literary review. On Saturday, May 18, 1844, *Journal* readers found a short article called "Curious Indian Traditions." "Some two hundred miles in the interior of the republic of Texas," the piece begins, "where the flat interminable prairies have ceased, the rolling country has commenced, and the evergreen summits of the verdant and flowery hills

Generations of Austin residents and visitors have enjoyed Barton Springs' cool water. *Author's collection.*

are in sight, was built not long since, on the very skirt of the territory of the fiercest and most turbulent Indian tribes, a small town to which the name Austin was given."

That, of course, constituted old news in Texas. Austin had been founded in 1839 as the republic's capital. But the article did not have much more to say about Austin. The rest of the short item focused on what it called "Barton's Springs." "Not far from the town," the piece continued, "gushing from the broad fissure in the rocky base of a hill, is a pure and delicious fountain, known as Barton's Springs...Surrounded on all sides by rocks or lofty trees, interminable groves of which branch off on three sides, it does not feel the effect of the sun's rays but during a very short period of the afternoon, when, through a large opening between certain lofty and stately cedars, the beams of the great luminary fall upon the spring, and gild its parking and virgin water with every tint of the rainbow."

That period of luminescence lasted only about forty-five minutes, the article says. Though short-lived, the effect must have been striking. In fact, the interaction of low-angle sunlight and water as clear as glass gave birth to what the *Journal* article labeled a "most curious" and long-forgotten Indian legend.

"In ages gone by," the article explains, "during a severe and terrible storm...a more than usually gorgeous rainbow was driven along with such force against the base of the hill from whence the spring gushes, as to shiver the rocks, and give place until the water which instantly welled forth."

The legend held that "the rainbow received equal damage with the more durable material, and being shattered to pieces, the fragments...mingled with the fountains, and caused the prismatic colours which, though brought out by the sun, are ever resident in the translucent body of the fountain; and the tints of the rainbow were blent with the wave."

Readers enjoying that colorful word picture must have found the end of the article jarring: "Both town and fountain are now abandoned to the aborigines, the war with Mexico having so weakened the resources of government as to render them incapable of defending their infant capital from the assaults of the Indian marauder."

While Austin languished as a virtual ghost town until Mexican military forces gave up on an attempt to reclaim their nation's lost territory, Barton Springs bubbled on, outlasting that trouble and everything since then. In time, Austin lived up to something else the *Edinburgh Journal* had printed: "It gave every prospect of becoming one of the most populous and active, as it is the most lovely city in this exceedingly picturesque and beautiful country."

TEXAS'S FIRST PUBLIC SCHOOL

Austin being the capital of Texas, all the laws dealing with major aspects of public education are made there. But the city has another distinction when it comes to teaching children: it had the first school in the state built entirely with public funds. That institution, the Austin Grade School, was dedicated on October 28, 1876. Built of stone, the three-story school had twelve classrooms and accommodated two hundred pupils. Public funds built the school, but the money to run it came from a combination of state dollars and tuition paid by parents. The state money was only sufficient to support the school four months out of the academic year, with tuition covering the rest.

The children who attended the school received a better education than many Texas kids, but they had to abide by some pretty tough rules by modern standards. According to a list of rules developed shortly after the school opened:

> *Pupils may not leave their seats without permission.*
> *Pupils may not communicate with each other in any way.*
> *In the morning, the male pupils will enter through the center door and the females through the side doors.*

Opened in 1876, Pease Elementary is Texas's oldest public school. *Photo by the author.*

At lunch time, the males and the females will be kept separate.
The use of tobacco in any form is strictly prohibited.
Pupils who arrive before nine and engage in sports unfit themselves for
study. Such pupils must go to their classroom and enter their studies.

School, as one of the rules indicates, began at 9:00 a.m. and ran to 4:00 p.m., with a one-hour lunch break. Boys attended classes on the third floor, girls on the second.

While the rules were strict compared to what school students must abide by today, some issues from the 1870s still sound pretty familiar. That's particularly true of this early entry in the minutes of the Austin School Board: "We find the teachers, while not complaining, embarrassed because of their meager salaries." Indeed, a teacher's salary in 1876 ranged from $70 a month for the person who taught the first graders to $100 a month for fourth-grade teachers and the principal.

As Austin grew and other schools had to be built, school officials renamed the Austin Grade School the West Austin School. It turned out pupils versed in reading, writing, composition, spelling, literature, geography, arithmetic, algebra, physiology, chemistry and Latin.

Not quite two decades after its doors opened for the first time, the school burned to the ground on May 28, 1896. Someone had poured oil inside the lower floor and torched it. An arsonist had succeeded in destroying a building, but his malicious deed did not change the city's feelings about the importance of public education. The school was rebuilt with two additional rooms. It continued to be known as the West Austin School until August 8, 1902, when it was renamed in honor of former Governor E.M. Pease, who had signed the bill spelling out Texas's public school system in 1854.

Pease Elementary School has been added to and remodeled several times over the intervening years, but it's still open—the oldest continually operated public school in Texas. Since 1958, it has been the only elementary school in Austin to which any student can transfer. It has only two classes per grade, which as the school's website says, "creates a close, friendly, and old-fashioned community school feeling."

And these days, girls and boys get to go to school together.

A Room for the Night

Honest Abe? Lincoln Slept Here?

"Hotel Where Lincoln Stayed Still Operating" reads the headline on the yellowed 1950 newspaper clipping. That a hotel might still be in business nearly a century after Abraham Lincoln spent the night in one of its rooms would not be particularly remarkable in Illinois—say Springfield—or Washington. But the "Lincoln slept here" assertion appeared in a Texas newspaper and referred to a historic hostelry in New Braunfels. Honest Abe? Lincoln in Texas?

First, some background. The hotel stands across from New Braunfels's town plaza at the corner of Seguin and San Antonio Streets and for much of its life was known as the Plaza. Built of limestone and cedar in 1851 by Adolph Nauendorf, the two-story structure was offered to Comal County for use as a courthouse in 1852. Balking at the $3,000 asking price, county commissions said no thanks.

Jacob Schmitz, one of the German immigrants who had founded the town in 1845, bought the property in 1858. Since at least 1854, he had been operating a stagecoach stop nearby on Seguin Street that he called the Guadalupe Hotel. Continuing under the same name at the new location, in 1873 he added a third floor and renamed the hotel for himself. New Braunfels being a good day's horseback ride from San Antonio and two days by wagon or stagecoach, the Schmitz Hotel saw a lot of business.

New Braunfels's old Schmitz Hotel opened in 1854. *Author's collection.*

In 1854, Frederick Law Olmsted, who would go on to design Central Park in New York, hit town on his tour of Texas. "There was nothing wanting," he later wrote of Schmitz's hotel when it was at its original location. After describing the pink-walled main room, he raved about the meal he had: "Excellent soup, two courses of meat (neither of them pork and neither of them fried), two vegetables, compote of peaches, coffee with milk, wheat bread, and beautiful sweet butter."

Eighteen years later, the poet Sidney Lanier spent a night at the hotel. "We arrived just at night-fall," he wrote, "found a large clean German town, with all manner of evidence of German thrift on every hand, through which we passed to the hotel, where mine host, a large-framed and seemingly large-souled German, was ready with a chair for the ladies to step on [presumably as they alighted from the stagecoach that stopped at the hotel]."

Like most innkeepers, Schmitz kept a guest register in a large bound book. Over the years, in addition to Olmsted and Lanier, numerous notables—from military officers to political figures like Sam Houston—lodged at the hotel. One of the guests was Jefferson Davis, U.S. secretary of war before he became president of the Confederate States of America.

And if the Schmitz's guest register is to be believed, the man who would be Jefferson's polar opposite during the Civil War also enjoyed the hotel's hospitality at some point between its opening and his election as the nation's sixteenth president. But if Lincoln ever came to Texas, much less the Schmitz Hotel in New Braunfels, the trip is a part of his well-examined life yet to be explored. If he did visit Texas, it would have been at some point between the time the hotel opened and 1860, when he ran for the presidency. Had Lincoln come to Texas after then, we'd be reading distinctly different American history books, since he was persona non grata with most Texans even prior to his election.

Lincoln never had much money, and travel back then wasn't easy. A review of his life's story suggests the closest he ever got to Texas was New Orleans, which he visited in 1831 when Louisiana's neighbor to the west was still a province of Mexico. Not that the future Great Emancipator didn't know about Texas, which by the time Lincoln got elected to Congress in 1847 had become the twenty-eighth state. As a freshman lawmaker, Lincoln pulled no punches in his criticism of President James K. Polk and the war with Mexico that began in the spring of 1846.

More than likely, at some point in the late 1850s as the tall, thin lawyer from Illinois became better known as an eloquent opponent of slavery, some unknown traveler thought it funny to scribble Lincoln's name in the Schmitz register. In later years, people more familiar with the president's name than his background accepted it as fact that he had visited Texas before the Civil War.

By the summer of 1950, when the story claiming Lincoln had stayed in New Braunfels ran in the *Austin American*, the hotel had become the Plaza. P.E. Short and his wife owned and operated it. "I wish Abraham Lincoln could come back and see the changes time and people have made since… Jacob Schmitz build the hotel," Mrs. Short told Comal County historian Oscar Haas, who wrote the newspaper article on the Plaza and Lincoln's supposed stay there.

The Plaza remained in business until 1961, finally closing after more than a century. The New Braunfels Conservation Society bought the old building in 1969 to keep it from being razed, and more recently, it has been remodeled and opened as a vacation and short-term rental property. If you visit, ask for the Lincoln bedroom.

THE ANTLERS HOTEL

On May 8, 1901, the *Austin Daily Statesman* ran a display ad that proclaimed, "May Day Excursion and Christening of the Antlers at Kingsland Under Auspices Austin Lodge B.P.O.E. (Benevolent and Protective Order of the Elks)."

At a roundtrip fare of $1.50, a special Austin and Northwestern train would leave the Capital City at 8:30 a.m. on May 15, reaching the Llano County community at the juncture of the Colorado and Llano Rivers three hours later. The return train would depart the Kingsland station at 8:00 p.m. for an 11:00 p.m. Austin arrival.

When the big day arrived, the *Statesman*'s Watters Park (an Austin and Northwestern stop just north of the city) correspondent took the trip, likely courtesy of the railroad in exchange for publicity. Not surprisingly, the unnamed journalist had a great time. "All that the...developers of Kingsland have said about it—after allowing the usual discount for their poetic fancies—is warranted by the facts," he wrote the day after returning from the Hill Country junket. "The Austin and Northwestern Railway...built a hotel facing the depot which for size, architectural design and completeness in all its interior arrangements would do credit to a big city."

Named for early settler Martin King, Kingsland got a rail connection in 1892, when the Austin and Northwestern built a bridge across the Colorado and a spur line off its main line to Llano. The destruction of Austin's Lake McDonald dam in the spring of 1900, which left the Capital City without any significant recreational attraction (other than Barton Springs), must have played a role in convincing the railroad that Kingsland could become a tourist destination.

Named for the Antlers Hotel in Colorado Springs, the Kingsland hotel was dedicated as the headquarters of the ancient order of the Elks, "and members of that order will find it a home where they can certainly rely upon getting home comforts."

Kingsland's boosters could not tout the town as a great agricultural center, the Austin correspondent continued, "but when they claim that it is the one spot in Texas where those suffering from ill health and the worries of business and the suffocating effect of the polluted air of a crowded city can offset those evils, they verily speak the truth."

It's hard to imagine the Austin of 1901 being polluted, but at twice the Capital City's altitude above sea level, Kingsland had less humidity and cooler nights. And it was certainly plenty quiet.

Kingsland's Antlers Hotel was restored and reopened in the mid-1990s. *Photo by the author.*

Fishing was good either in the Colorado or Llano Rivers, and the hotel keeper—identified in the report only as Mrs. Carrington—laid out good groceries. As the newspaper writer put it, "The one unvarying verdict was: 'This is the best meal I ever ate at a public function.'"

Predicting that Kingsland would grow into a popular "health and pleasure resort," the newspaper writer went on to surmise that "as soon as the public learns the advantages of the place as a holiday resort there will be less traveling to northern points with not a fraction of Kingsland's attractions."

The hotel did do well as long as getting to Kingsland by train constituted the only easy way to make the trip, but with the development of automobile travel, business declined. Closed in 1923, the hotel was sold to Thomas H. Barrow, whose family kept it and used it as a private retreat that became all the more enjoyable after the Lower Colorado River Authority dammed the river and, in the process, transformed the old Antler Hotel into lakeside property.

Barbara Thomas, a librarian turned children's bookseller, bought the old hotel in 1993. She and her husband had intended to "fix it up and get out," but the fixing up took three years and a lot of work. To guard against erosion, the couple had three-ton granite blocks put in place with a crane along the property's 1,500-foot lakefront. In addition to restoring the hotel, they moved an old log cabin from property across the lake to the site of another cabin that had stood on their property.

In the spring of 1995, about the time the place had become livable, their Sandy Harbor lake house flooded. The Thomases moved into the Antlers and tried to live there, but they had so many guests it began to feel like the hotel it used to be. On top of that, people showed up thinking it was a hotel. So the couple went with the flow and opened it to the public in 1996. They built a two-story annex with a conference room next door and began adding a collection of historic railroad cars that they transformed into rentable rooms.

Now, more than a century after the Antlers first opened its doors, the booming Capital City does occasionally have polluted air. But the restored hotel remains a great place to forget the worries of business.

JOHNSON CITY'S PEARL HOTEL

Depending on traffic flow, Johnson City is only about a half hour's drive from Austin. That makes it hard to picture what travel must have been like when the trip from the Capital City to Johnson City took a day and a half by horse, even longer by wagon. The town had no rail connection, and the road between Austin and Fredericksburg, on which Johnson City sits about mid-point, did not get paved until 1924.

If the isolation of the small town where future President Lyndon B. Johnson grew up is difficult to grasp, the importance of a comfortable place to spend the night is much easier to understand. For $2.50, a weary horseback, wagon or stagecoach traveler could get a room, a bath and one meal at the Pearl Hotel, a two-story frame building with a long, shady front porch and a covered veranda upstairs.

James Polk Johnson, L.B.J.'s grandfather's nephew, donated in 1879 the 320-acre tract of land that became the community named in his honor. The new town needed a hotel, which Johnson had built around 1882. He named it after his daughter, Pearl. The hotel accommodated cowboys and traveling salesmen, but visitors seldom had trouble getting a room. Business picked up in 1890, when Johnson City became the county seat, supplanting Blanco. Unfortunately, Johnson had not lived to see that, dying at forty in 1885. A one-story addition was connected to the hotel in 1905 and for a time was used as a school, the town's first.

Dave G. Adams bought the property in 1929, added a coat of stucco to the exterior and put up a sign that said "Adams Hotel." Though he chose to go with his surname rather than a daughter's first name, two of his daughters were born in the hotel.

The hotel stayed in business off and on through L.B.J.'s political ascendancy, finally closing in 1969, the same year Johnson left the White House and came home to his ranch on the Pedernales.

For a time after that, the old hotel served as the town's city hall. But when the city moved out, no one else proved particularly eager to move in. The building remained vacant, falling into worse shape day by day. After standing empty for fifteen years, the hotel had been invaded by trumpet vines and other vegetation. A tree even grew inside the old kitchen, and squirrels nested in the attic.

In short, the old hotel didn't look like much in the spring of 2000 when Morris and Elissa Johnson first checked it out. But the Driftwood couple saw possibilities. Newly retired—he from a long career with Texaco, she after twenty-six years of teaching first graders in Austin—they were interested in a place to sell antiques and crafts.

The Johnsons found owner Kent Smith definitely interested in selling, but only with a certain stipulation. "He said he wouldn't sell it to us if we were going to tear it down," Johnson said. "We told him our plans, and he kinda took up with us."

On April 13, 2000, the couple closed on the sale. It took them eighteen months to bring the Pearl back to life. Johnson did much of the work himself, assisted by three hired hands. He traveled all over Texas, Louisiana and part of Arkansas looking for old glass panes for use in repairing partially broken windows, as well as for five full windows that needed replacing. Fittingly, they painted the exterior—still stuccoed—a pearl gray. The couple pulled up multiple layers of carpet and linoleum to expose the original hardwood floors. "There was a layer of newspapers from 1928, linoleum, a layer of newspapers from the 1940s, another layer of linoleum," Mrs. Johnson said. "Upstairs, there were a couple of layers of carpet on top of the linoleum."

Debris from the remodeling project filled two industrial-sized metal trash containers and uncounted plastic garbage bags, she said.

About the only thing they didn't find in the makeover was a ghost. "If this place is haunted, I haven't made any of them mad yet," Johnson laughed.

Mrs. Johnson, however, did have one real-world problem to deal with. She wanted to bake and sell scones in the tearoom she envisioned, but she couldn't find a recipe. Finally, in a book owned by an elderly aunt, she discovered an old recipe for "Queen's Biscuits."

The Pearl's grand reopening was in November 2001. These days, its eleven rooms are used to display the antiques and crafts they have for sale, items ranging from homemade jelly to unique lamps. The rear addition, once a school, is now Mrs. Johnson's tearoom. She serves her homemade scones with Devonshire cream and preserves, finger sandwiches, fruit and tea.

Johnson City is still a small country town, but it's no longer isolated. Some of the Pearl's visitors have been from as far away as England, and they've pronounced Mrs. Johnson's scones the best they've ever eaten.

MYSTERIES AND COULD-HAVE-BEENS

IS TEXAS'S FIRST ANGLO GRAVE IN LAMPASAS COUNTY?

A thunderstorm growing darker by the minute hungrily sucked moisture-rich air from the south, the resulting strong wind shaking the blue cloth tied around the state historical marker folks had come to dedicate at Lampasas County's Longmeadow Cemetery.

His gray straw cowboy hat seated solidly on his head, eighty-eight-year-old Arlee Claud Gowen stood before an assemblage of relatives and a few guests with his back facing the soon-to-be-unveiled metal marker. Clutching a yellow-tipped microphone in one hand and the text of his remarks in the other, he put things into perspective.

"When Abraham Lincoln spoke at Gettysburg, he referred to the area as hallowed ground," the longtime Lubbock resident began. "Lincoln referred to the nation as then having 'four score and seven years.' The tenure of this cemetery is now 'ten score and eighteen years.'"

A former newspaper reporter-printer and decorated World War II veteran, Gowen ranks as dean of a group of tenacious genealogists belonging to a branch of the Cox family (no relation to author) that has traced its Texas roots deeper than even the most water-starved mesquite. Many of their forebears are buried in this small rural cemetery, a fenced graveyard accessible only by an unpaved private road. In Lampasas

Susan Cox of Dallas (no relation to author) near the old Cox family cemetery in Lampasas County. No one knows who piled these stones, but they are believed to date to the late 1700s. *Photo by the author.*

for their annual reunion, members of the Brandywine Crucible—an organization of people named Cox and various other surnames— attended the marker dedication on May 21, 2011.

While its exact location is unknown, the first burial in or near this cemetery eight miles east of Lampasas occurred in 1793. And it may well be the oldest Anglo burial in Texas. Nearby stand remnants of stone fences thought to date back to the 1700s as well, possibly built to trap or corral wild horses.

Only a decade after the Revolutionary War, a party of American mustangers led by Virginia-born Thomas Isaac Cox came to the vast plains of Spanish Texas hunting wild horses. They encountered an Indian war party and succeeded in repulsing them, but Cox's nephew, sixteen-year-old William Charles Bybee, caught an arrow in his chest. Someone broke the feathered shaft and extracted the arrowhead, but everyone must have known the teenager wouldn't make it. After suffering through the night, begging for water, Bybee died the following morning. It was his seventeenth birthday— July 4, 1793.

"His companions dug his grave at the foot of a large post oak tree and wrapped his body in his blanket," Gowen continued. "They carried large limestone slates from the fence surrounding the immense horse trap nearby and placed them on top of his grave."

The youth's grandfather, James Christopher Cox, chopped three diagonal slashes on the tree to mark the grave. Gowen said he had interviewed Joe Burton Cox Sr., who grew up on the ranch surrounding the cemetery, before his death. "He…recalled seeing this tree with its three slashes when he was a boy," Gowen said. "Later he wrote a history of this cemetery and mentioned thirty-seven burials here."

A story connected to the last person buried in Longmeadow Cemetery circles around to its long-ago first burial. Martha Jane Bybee married Pleasant C. Cox, who in 1856 came to Texas to homestead on the land where William Bybee, her father's brother, had been buried the previous century. When he learned she would be going to Texas with her new husband to settle where her relatives had trapped horses in the 1700s, her father asked her to find and care for Bybee's grave. She did that, planted flowers and kept those flowers and their successors watered until her own death fifty-six years later. On a bitterly cold day in February 1912, her family buried her in the cemetery. Ten years later, the Coxes sold the ranch, and the cemetery became overgrown.

One of Martha Jane's sons, John Thomas Cox, later rode as a Texas Ranger. According to family lore, he once observed that the old cemetery held the remains of citizens of six different nations that at one time or another held control of Texas. "Burials were made under the flag of Spain until 1799, the tricolor of France until 1803, the flag of Mexico until 1836, the flag of the Republic of Texas until 1845, the flag of the Confederate States of America until 1865 and the Stars and Stripes of the United States until the present," Gowen said.

The youngest occupant of the cemetery is Joseph "Buck" Cox, a brother of the Ranger who first pointed out the multinational aspect of the family plot. Not quite four, Buck died on May 5, 1872. "His death came as a result of a concussion received by butting his head against a wall in a temper tantrum," Gowen said.

Of the known burials in the cemetery, only a handful are marked by headstones. In 2001, the Coxes got Dr. John Dunbar, a Baylor University geologist, to survey the cemetery with ground-penetrating radar. He located twenty-one other likely graves, now marked by stakes.

Among the known but unmarked graves are those of Charlie Boyd, a cowboy who rode for the legendary cattleman "Shanghai" Pierce, and another waddy known only as "Stumpy" Watson. According to Gowen, on December 10, 1874, the two men got into a row that escalated into a gunfight. When the black powder smoke cleared, both lay mortally wounded. Folks carried them to the Cox house, where Martha Jane nursed them for a week and a half. Despite her best efforts, Boyd died at sunrise on December 22. "When she told 'Stumpy' that Charlie had died," Gowen said, "he replied, 'Good, now I can die in peace.'" And that's just what he proceeded to do.

Austin, Texas, Could Have Been Lamar, Texas

While naming the Capital City after the impresario who brought the first Anglo settlers to Texas certainly is fitting, the city of Austin just as well could have been named Lamar in honor of a Georgia newspaperman with a penchant for poetry. Mirabeau B. Lamar came to Texas in 1835 intending to write its history. He never got around to that project (though he did gather a lot of material that is still useful to scholars today), but he certainly had a hand in making some of Texas's history.

Lamar joined the Texian Army as a private but soon rose to the rank of colonel. He distinguished himself in the Battle of San Jacinto, the brief but bloody fight that assured Texas's independence from Mexico, and that caught Sam Houston's eye. When Houston ran for president, Lamar got elected as his vice president.

The two men, each with strong personalities but vastly different philosophies, soon fell out politically. Because the Republic of Texas's constitution forbade a president from serving two consecutive terms, Lamar ran for office when Houston's term expired. Houston campaigned against him, but Lamar gained the office despite that.

The main reason Lamar is important to Austin is that it probably would not have been chosen as the capital had it not been for Lamar. If Sam Houston had his way, the bayou city named in his honor would have continued as the capital of the republic. Had it not been for Lamar, that might well have happened.

A second significant impact Lamar had on Austin was in championing the need for higher education in Texas. The former president had long been in his grave by the time Austin became home to the University of Texas in 1883, but Lamar is credited as the father of education in the

Top: Marble statue of Stephen F. Austin by sculptress Elisabet Ney. *Author's collection.*

Bottom: Republic of Texas President Mirabeau B. Lamar deserves better recognition. After all, he made Austin the capital city. *Author's collection.*

Lone Star State. For years, freshman college students in Texas had to memorize this observation by Lamar: "Education is the guardian genius of democracy. It is the only dictator that free men recognize, and the only ruler that free men require."

Lamar is way underrated in Texas history and all but forgotten, even in Austin. True, one of the Capital City's busiest north–south thoroughfares is named in his honor, along with a middle school. But where is the Mirabeau B. Lamar Library or even a statue erected in his honor? (There is a Lamar statue in Richmond, but not Austin.) There are state office buildings named for Sam Houston, Stephen F. Austin, Lorenzo de Zavala, William B. Travis, John H. Reagan, Price Daniel, Bill Clements and others. But where is the Mirabeau B. Lamar State Building?

Back in the early 1960s, despite the suggestion of a prominent Austinite well familiar with Texas history, the citizens of Austin couldn't even bring themselves to name their beautiful city lake in Lamar's honor. It would be hard to come up with a name any more pedestrian than they did: Town Lake. (Eventually, it was renamed Lady Bird Lake.)

Lamar isn't even buried in Austin's State Cemetery. His remains lie in the old city cemetery in Richmond. Statewide, there is a county in North Texas named in Lamar's honor. A ghost town in Aransas County was known as Lamar. A Liberty ship constructed during World

War II was named the *Mirabeau B. Lamar*. Houston has a high school named for Lamar, and at least a couple of Texas cities have a Lamar elementary school. There's even a golf course with its tenth hole named in Lamar's honor. Finally, there is Lamar University in Beaumont.

Still, it seems like Lamar deserves more.

DIGGING UP A MYSTERY

Newly elected governor Jim Ferguson was giving Austin's two daily newspapers plenty to write about as the legislative session progressed that February 1915, not to mention the war in Europe and bandit troubles on the border with Mexico. But on February 28 that year, the *Austin American* ran a two-column, inside story that offered its readers something different to think about. The day before, the story related, Joe Macken had been excavating on the east side of Congress Avenue between Seventh and Eighth Streets as part of the foundation work for a new theater to be built at the site.

About ten feet down, Macken saw something in the dirt that looked out of place. Picking it up, he discovered it was a round piece of copper, about two inches across and weighing maybe five ounces. Cleaning off the dirt clinging to the object, he saw the words: "State of Louisiana to Major General Zachary Taylor." Beneath that legend was the seal of Louisiana.

On the other side of the medal, he found an embossed reproduction of the Battle of Buena Vista, the turning point of the Mexican War in 1847. The battle, the war and Taylor's career all are matters of copious record, but how a medal honoring the general ended up underground in Austin was a mystery in 1915 and still is.

The newspaper noted that the theater (now known as the Paramount) was going up at the site of the old Avenue Hotel, once the city's prime hostelry and stagecoach stop. The anonymous journalist theorized that somehow, the medal had been lost in the garden once located behind the hotel. "It is believed by old settlers that the relic was carried by one of the Mexican war soldiers, who was probably entrusted with the keeping of the medal by General Taylor," the newspaper article continued. "He, while enjoying the comforts of the garden near the hotel, probably became over engulfed in beverage [read, drunk] and dropped the heavy copper disk."

That might have been the case, but the hotel did not open until 1850, a couple of years after the war ended. More likely the medal being where it was had more to do with the fact that the Republic of Texas's Department of War building had been there prior to the Avenue Hotel. Even after Texas statehood—the triggering factor in the war that brought about the fight at Buena Vista—the building probably had been used by the military.

It also is hard to imagine that the medal found in Austin was *the* medal presented to the general. While an Internet search did not bring up any sites mentioning a medal given to Taylor by Louisiana, the Smithsonian Institution's website has an image of a gold medal awarded to the general by a grateful U.S. Congress for his leadership at Buena Vista. The site says the medal also was struck in

An old copper medal found in Austin in 1915 commemorated Mexican War hero and future President Zachary Taylor. *Author's collection.*

a less-precious metal. That being the case, it likely went to other officers involved in the battle. That probably was true of the Louisiana medal as well, but the vast interconnectedness of the Internet is silent on the subject.

No matter its provenance, the medal found in downtown Austin, the 1915 article went on, "is highly prized by the finder and will likely be placed on exhibition by him in a show window during the next few days."

The legislature being in session, Senator C.A. Nugent of Conroe read the story of the find with more than ordinary interest. The state lawmaker was a great-nephew of the general, who had been elected to the presidency on the heels of his success in Mexico.

Nugent, whose great-grandmother on his mother's side was Taylor's sister, told the *American* that he owned a flint arrowhead picked up by Taylor at the Battle of Lake Okeechobee earlier in his military career. That fight came during the Seminole War in Florida, where Taylor began establishing his reputation as a "Rough and Ready" army officer. The senator said he was thinking about donating the war souvenir to the Library of Congress. Who knows what became of that arrowhead or Taylor's medal from Louisiana?

At least one mystery connected to Taylor, however, did eventually get solved. For years, speculation had been afoot that President Taylor, who died in 1850, had been poisoned. In 1991, his descendants agreed to the exhumation of his body so samples could be taken for DNA testing. That testing revealed the level of arsenic in his body had been normal, supporting the official story that he had died of gastric difficulties.

But the lesser mystery endures of how the buried medal struck in Taylor's honor, now probably in the hands of some collector or museum, ended up ten feet below ground in downtown Austin.

DARE DEVIL ROGERS

Who was Dare Devil Rogers? The world's mightiest Internet search engine is stumped by the question, finding no mention anywhere in cyber space of anyone by that name. No matter his given name or where he was from or what became of him, Dare Devil Rogers must have been quite a character. And definitely not claustrophobic.

During the Depression, as the people of the nation collectively dug deep into their pockets and often came up with nothing, Dare Devil dug his own grave time after time, town after town. Not that he had a suicidal bent. At least not overtly. Dare Devil made his living by imitating the dead. His shtick was to have himself buried alive to promote some event or business. He coped with a poor economy by simply laying low—six feet low.

Dare Devil capitalized on man's ancient fear of being buried alive—and his fascination in hearing or reading stories about instances of premature burial—by turning it into a traveling promotional act. For a fee, he would listen to a sound most people never hear: dirt hitting the outside of a coffin lid.

On January 23, 1937, Dare Devil was interred in his special coffin in a vacant lot just south of the Tower Café on South Congress Avenue in Austin. "He will stay in this underground grave for ten days," the long-defunct *Austin Daily Dispatch* reported in a five-paragraph, page-one story on January 27, four days into his planned ten-day burial.

The story continued: "Spectators looked down the metal tube that exposes his face through the week-end with awe, and bewilderment. A prize has been offered to any one catching him asleep during the interlude he is underground." Prize-crazy Austinites tried hard to catch him asleep, even visiting the grave in the dead of the night hoping to find him making ZZZZZs.

Sleep, of course, is not the only issue for those driven to an early grave. For obvious natural reasons, Rogers eschewed food while buried. He kept

"Grave" of "Country Bill" White while he lay at rest in 1968 at Austin's Chief Drive-In. *Photo by the author.*

himself going, the newspaper reported, by "drinking a bottle of popular beer ever hour." (Given that level of orally administered "embalming fluid," his special coffin must also have had some special plumbing as well.)

To accommodate around-the-clock viewing, Dare Devil's graveside was bathed in light at night. Even with illumination above, it must have gotten chilly underground. Just how he kept warm during winter gigs was not revealed in the frustratingly brief newspaper coverage.

"The breaking of the inclement weather indicates that hundreds more will view the 'Dare Devil,'" the newspaper concluded.

Dare Devil may have drawn a crowd and helped the Tower Café sell more hamburgers, but he couldn't top the master at being buried alive— Harry Houdini. The magician not only allowed himself to be buried, but he would also proceed to escape. The only interest Dare Devil had in escape was getting out of town with as much money as possible.

Thirty-one years after Dare Devil Rogers rested in peace in Austin for a few days, another "underground" entertainer hit town—a fellow who called himself Country Bill White. In 1968, White had himself buried in front of the screen at the old Chief Drive-In at Lamar and Koenig. Like Dare Devil, he had a viewing tube so visitors could see how he was doing down under before it got dark enough to see that night's feature film. Unlike Dare Devil, Country Bill had a telephone in his coffin and was more than happy to be interviewed by local radio stations. After lying down on the job for the required number of days, just as Dare Devil had done three decades before, Country Bill moved on to another early but temporary grave.

Ghost Towns

The Athens That Never Was

Somewhere in northern Travis County or southern Williamson County is the site of a long-dead dream, a "delightful" community that never was.

Anyone who keeps up with the news knows Austin's a tough town for developers, despite its growth rate. Building a box store or a new subdivision is not guaranteed in a city where the popular slogan on T-shirts and gimme caps is "Keep Austin Weird," especially if the populace perceives a proposed project as a threat to the environment. But back in the nineteenth century, residents of the Capital City stood four square in favor of development. Even then, however, translating a concept into reality could be tricky.

In his classic book, *The Texan Santa Fe Expedition*, journalist George Wilkins Kendall tells the story of the ill-conceived 1841 Texas venture to New Mexico, an attempt by Republic of Texas President Mirabeau B. Lamar to establish trade with Santa Fe, a city with an overland link to St. Louis in the United States. Mexico still considered New Mexico its territory, so the Texans ended up in a dank Mexican prison. The story of the Texas incursion in New Mexico is an epic folly, but Kendall, who participated in the expedition, seems not to have been able to resist any anecdote he came across. By all rights, his telling of the short-but-intriguing story of a ghost town that never had a ghost of a chance in the first place should have been cut by some space-minded editor. Fortunately for history, the three paragraphs Kendall devoted to the tale survived, which is a lot more than can be said of a city envisioned as the educational center of Texas.

The expedition left Austin in mid-June 1841. On their first day, the men traveled about twenty miles from the Capital City to a camp on Brushy Creek in present Williamson County. Along the way, Kendall passed the site of a paper ghost town, though it is not clear whether he heard the story in 1841 or at some point prior to his book's publication some years later. Kendall's description of the town's location, at least to a twenty-first-century reader, is equally vague: "To the left of the road, at the distance of some mile and a half or two miles, is a high and delightful situation." The road he referred to probably lies beneath the asphalt of North Lamar Boulevard in Austin, a piece of paving that roughly follows the route of the old military road to North Texas. Kendall's reference to a "high and delightful situation" must refer to the hills of the Balcones Escarpment, which are about that distance from modern Lamar Boulevard. He never said how far north of Austin the "delightful situation" lay.

As has been the case with many a development since then, "highly-coloured plans were got out, and on paper, at least, a more flourishing place never existed." The drawing depicted "colleges and squares, city halls and penitentiaries, public walks and public houses."

His future city clearly intended as a cultural center, the unnamed developer did not waste time on originality in coming up with a name. His coming oasis of learning in Texas would be Athens.

To look at the developer's fanciful engraved vision of Athens, Texas, Kendall went on, "a man could almost imagine he heard the carriages rattling over the pavements, and the busy hum which denotes the large and thriving city." The would-be developer built a house for himself on the property and "made some other and expensive improvements on the premises."

So what went wrong? For one thing, as Kendall wrote, Athens lacked "only all the essentials to support a large population." For another, the developer apparently did not realize he did not have 100 percent local support for his project.

One day, digging what would be Athens's first well, the developer and several of his slaves found themselves surrounded by Comanches. The Indians drove them away, the landowner "narrowly escaping with his life." The man gave up his house, his uncompleted well, the other improvements he had made and, most important, his dream. According to Kendall, the man never returned.

The large and thriving city the developer had envisioned would come, but its name was Austin, not Athens.

BLUFFTON: UNDERWATER GHOST TOWN

Isaac "Ike" B. Maxwell had been on the road so long he had taken to talking to his mule. Born in Tennessee in 1837 and raised in Arkansas, some months earlier the seventeen-year-old had saddled a mule and started riding southwest toward Texas. He didn't stop until he got to the Colorado River in Burnet County. Looking at the high limestone cliffs across the river in what would become Llano County, he told his mule, "This is the place I've dreamed of all my life."

Whether his mule had an opinion on the subject is not recorded, but Maxwell was ready to establish roots.

He settled about a half-mile from the future site of Bluffton, a town he and one of his shirttail kinsmen, Bob Davis, founded in 1854. When a petition went to Washington in 1858 requesting a post office for Bluffton, a town he named either for Bluffton, Arkansas, or for the bluffs on the river, Maxwell's name was prominently signed. Maxwell also had a hand in organizing Llano County.

Once the new political subdivision had its first county clerk, Maxwell purchased the first marriage license issued in the county. And he got his money's worth out of the document, going on to father nineteen children and outliving (no wonder) three wives.

View of Buchanan Dam site early in the construction process. *Author's collection.*

Fragments of Depression glass found at the site of Old Bluffton when the Lake Buchanan water level fell dramatically during the 2009 Texas drought. *Photo by Hallie Cox.*

Located near an easy river crossing, Bluffton became a stopping place for stagecoaches and horseback travelers. When the water ran high, the owner of a thirty-foot flatboat ferried horses and wagons across the Colorado, the minimum fee being a quarter for a horse and rider.

Settlers feared hostile Indians more than high water. Maxwell rode with a party of citizens who trailed Indians after a raid on July 6, 1859. For the next fifteen years, Indians stole every horse they found loose or unguarded in the area. No dummy, Maxwell devised a theft prevention system that worked so well others soon adopted the technique. What he did was stuff an old coat with grass, stick a hat on it and prop the "scare Indian" next to a stump. Soon many livestock owners in the county had begun making what came to be called "Maxwell dummies."

By the time the Indian threat ended in the mid-1870s, Bluffton had become a substantial town with a hotel, a church, a number of stores, two blacksmith shops and four saloons. The community's progress suffered a major setback when some cowpoke's overindulgence at one of those establishments led to a fire that spread rapidly through the town. The 1883 blaze, as one writer later put it, destroyed just about everything but the spirit of the townspeople. Unperturbed, the citizenry and business community built a new town about a mile from the ashes of the first Bluffton.

Maxwell, meanwhile, gained election to the legislature in 1884. In one of his more significant achievements, he played a role in convincing state officials to use granite from Burnet County rather than limestone from Indiana in the construction of the new capitol.

For Bluffton residents, a fact of life nearly as enduring as granite was the periodic problem of flooding in their community as well as farther down the river. Far-sighted folks for years had talked about damming the river for flood control and to generate electricity through hydropower. A private effort to construct a dam failed, but federal money made available during the New Deal proved sufficient to get the job done.

When all the engineering work for the long-contemplated dam was completed in the mid-1930s, residents of Bluffton received some hard news—the town would be inundated by the new lake. Once the lake reached full elevation, Bluffton would lie underwater some two miles from shore.

The most tangible evidence of inundated Old Bluffton is its relocated cemetery. *Photo by the author.*

In the mid-'30s, as workers poured concrete at the dam site and laborers just happy to have a job in hard times used handsaws to denude the landscape in the future lake bed of oaks and cedars, the Lower Colorado River Authority paid to have the occupants of the Bluffton Cemetery exhumed for reburial at a new site well above the future shoreline. The town's living residents soon followed, settling what for a time they called New Bluffton, the seventy-two-year-old community's third incarnation.

One of the first burials in the new cemetery had been Bluffton's pioneer settler, "Ike" Maxwell. Having lived for ninety-four years, he died in 1931 while the dam that would cover his old homestead slowly took shape.

Completed in 1937, the new dam created a lake thirty-two miles long and eight miles wide. As expected, the new impoundment inundated what remained of Bluffton. The sprawling lake also necessitated the moving of State Highway 29, which connected Burnet and Llano. But the new route did not pass through New Bluffton, stunting its chance for any growth.

"Old Bluffton, Old Bluffton, for thee I sigh," one old-timer had written as residents adjusted to the idea that their hometown would soon be buried under many feet of water. "When the big lake is finished it will be a sight I will love to see…the great big dam with its great white wall, but the memories of Old Bluffton will rise above them all."

Periodic droughts occasionally expose the scattered foundations of the normally submerged ghost town, but these days, even most of the memories are gone.

KATEMCY

Early-day Texans and Comanches were not always trying to kill each other; it just seemed like it. The Republic of Texas, and later the U.S. government, did execute a few peace treaties with the Indians, but the problem was more complicated than something a mere signature could fix. A well-meaning chief might agree to lasting peace, but in a culture built largely on raiding, bravery in battle and the number of horses a man owned, not every ambitious young man in his tribe was likely to go along with a written agreement of non-hostility. And not every Comanche headman, either.

One Comanche who did put his sign on a piece of paper and lived up to it was a Penateka chief named Katemoczy, who often camped along the San Saba River in the northwest corner of what would become Mason

This long-closed general store is about all that remains of Katemcy. *Photo by the author.*

County. German immigrant John Meusebach worked out that treaty with the Comanches in 1846, and it held. Because of that document, German settlers in the Hill Country, while not immune from Indian depredations, fared better than many other frontier Texans.

As Mason County began to settle up, some held the chief in high enough esteem to name one of their towns in his honor, though it was an afterthought. When settler Andrew Jackson Coots built a cabin in the area in the later 1870s, people started calling the community that developed around it Cootsville.

Dr. William F. Cowan and his wife moved to the area in 1879. Whether it was the doctor's idea or one of his two sons, the place came to be called Katemcy in misspelled honor of Chief Katemoczy. One of the doctor's sons, Alfred R. Cowan, donated land for the Katemcy town site around 1880. Four years later, he became Katemcy's first postmaster. One of seventeen post office towns in Mason County, Katemcy flourished until the mid-1920s. In its peak years, it had two drugstores, two general stores, two blacksmith shops, a barbershop, a business described as a "chili shack," three churches and a school with three teachers.

"We have two churches, and preaching every Sunday," someone from Katemcy wrote for the *Mason County News* in January 1887, "but we are liable to accidents here as elsewhere and want some good doctor [Dr. Cowan was getting up in years and no longer practicing medicine] who will not charge unreasonable for his services to come and make his home among us." In addition to a doctor, the town needed a "general merchandise business" that would "sell goods at a living price and buy our corn, cotton and coon skins."

Half of the letter was taken up with a plea for improved transportation. "We want," the writer continued, "and will have a public road to Mason or move our trade to Brady or Brownwood."

In fact, on the day this correspondent put words to paper, January 14, the able-bodied men of the community had worked on the road from Katemcy to Mason, a distance of twelve miles. Still, more improvements were needed. (This was long before pavement, of course.) The letter writer said a petition would be presented to the county commissioner's court "for a public road of the third class and we want to see Mason co-operate with us."

Indeed, the writer continued, Mason needed a good road as badly as Katemcy. Then the writer made his most prescient point of all: "If we do not get the roads now while the country is new, it will cost money to get them later."

For a time, the forerunner of Highway 87 from San Antonio to San Angelo passed through Katemcy, bringing with it just enough out-of-town business to keep the economy alive. But when state engineers relocated the highway about a mile to the west, the impact on Katemcy proved severe, and the town began a slow decline to just shy of ghost-town status.

One thing that has lasted, however, is a historical marker put up in 1967 at the site of what for years had been the smallest piece of state-owned land in Texas. Intended for use as a mini state park, the tract eventually went back to private ownership. Katemcy, meanwhile, has been virtually forgotten, along with an Indian chief who preferred peace to war.

GHOSTS

JAKE'S BRIDGE

Being a cotton farmer was not the easiest way to make a living, but if a man didn't mind working from can see to can't, he could get by and maybe save a little.

Texas farmers tilled the black soil to bring forth white fiber, battling the boil weevil and the vagaries of Texas weather to produce a crop each year. But some years, no matter how many hours a man and his family and hired hands put in grubbing and picking, forces beyond his control could suddenly reroute his life. When the price of cotton went down, all a man could do was hope the market rebounded next year. When it didn't rain enough to keep his plants alive, he could pray for more rain next season, providing it didn't all come at once in a flood.

But as the Depression began to worsen in the early 1930s, cotton didn't bounce back. In 1929, cotton brought 16.9 cents a pound. Two years later, the price had fallen to less than 6.0 cents. Many Central Texas farmers lost their land, their homes and, finally, their spirit.

Maybe that's what made Jake snap. No one seems to know his last name, but many people in Williamson County know about Jake. For whatever reason, according to the story, Jake killed his wife and two children. When the reality of what he had done set in, he took his own life as well, hanging himself from a back-road wooden bridge between Hutto and Pflugerville, near the Williamson-Travis County line.

Jake, now reputed to be a quite active ghost, started off as a struggling cotton farmer like these hardworking folks. *Author's collection.*

That's one story. Another has Jake being a young man who killed his parents, pushing the car containing their bodies off the rural bridge. Later, this story goes, Jake died in a house fire.

Whoever he was, and if he ever was, Jake seems not to have been a happy person. His spirit, some say, lingers around the bridge (since replaced by a more modern concrete structure) that figures in both versions of the tale.

Somewhere along the line, the story arose that Jake's ghost liked to mess with cars on the bridge, trying to push them off. Supposedly, if you stop your car on the bridge and shift into neutral, you can feel the vehicle begin to move. If your car happens to be dusty, the story continues, you'll find handprints on the back. Some claimed to have "proven" Jake's efforts to move their wheels by spreading flour on their trunks.

Those who like rational explanations for unusual phenomena have argued that the bridge must not be level, having just enough of a slope for a car to roll if it's not in gear. Since it's a relatively new bridge, that doesn't seem too likely.

Learning of the legend, one Central Texas resident decided to check it out. "We arrived around 1 a.m. and walked a very sturdy, level looking bridge," he wrote in an e-mail. "Then the ultimate test…we parked the car, put it in neutral and sure enough the car moved the entire bridge. What was strange was how the car felt. It didn't at all feel like a normal roll of a car on a grade—it felt like a force pushing it for sure. The car really moved faster and faster but we stopped as soon as we were at the end of it."

An old house in the vicinity of the bridge also is supposedly haunted by Jake. A website devoted to Texas ghost tales says visitors have reported hearing footsteps, children screaming and a voice yelling, "I am coming for you."

A variant of the Jake story has to do with a friendly ghost—or ghosts—given to moving vehicles off railroad tracks. The story occasionally grows around a particular grade crossing where a busload of children supposedly died when a train plowed into their bus. If a modern-day vehicle stops or stalls on the tracks, the story goes, the spirits of the children will push the vehicle to safety.

Retired Taylor journalism teacher Susan Komandosky remembers hearing the friendly ghost story attributed to a rail crossing in the Round Rock area, and a similar story is popular in San Antonio. (In the San Antonio case, someone did some research and found that a bus-train crash never occurred at the site of the supposed haunting. But the researcher found the telling of the tale dated to the late 1930s, when a bus-train crash in Utah received considerable newspaper coverage in the Alamo City.)

"Looking for Jake was a great way to get your date out in the country at night," Pflugerville resident Jeremy Boehm later recalled. "What better way to promote a spirit of closeness than to tell a spooky story and then comfort your scared date?"

Boehm says that if you ever go looking for Jake, be sure to check out the glowing tombstone in the Hutto Cemetery. According to Boehm, when you drive south on FM 1660 at night and approach the cemetery, one tombstone will appear to light up.

The perfect ending for this Central Texas folk tale would be to report that the solitary "glowing" grave marker belonged to someone named Jake, but that wouldn't be true. "It's just the way the graves are arranged," Boehm said. "None of the other graves catch the light when a car passes."

But no one has such a pat explanation for the stories about Jake.

GREER BUILDING GHOSTS

If Hubert Harvey hadn't fatally stabbed that young Austin man on Halloween night in 1916, he might have lived to see the fine new Texas Highway Department building go up where the Travis County Jail once stood. But that's not how it worked out. At 1:50 p.m. on August 23, 1918, Sheriff George Matthews sprang the trap on the gallows inside the jail, and Harvey paid for his crime at the end of a rope.

The thirty-four-year-old Harvey had the distinction of being the last of nine men legally hanged in the castle-like stone jail, built for $100,000 in 1876 at the corner of Eleventh and Brazos Streets—present location of the Dewitt C. Greer Building, headquarters of what is now the Texas Department of Transportation.

Who knows? Maybe Harvey's spirit has something to do with the mysterious footsteps and strange noises some TxDOT employees have reported hearing at night when the building's supposedly empty. But for anyone who believes in ghosts, there are plenty of suspects.

Austin's Greer Building is home to the Texas Department of Transportation and, some say, a few noisy ghosts. *Author's collection.*

John Wesley Hardin, Texas's deadliest nineteenth-century outlaw, cooled his heels in the still-new jail in 1877 until his transfer to the state prison in Huntsville. John Ringo, another famous outlaw, did some time in the Travis County slammer before moving west to Arizona. A more genteel inmate was William Sydney Porter, a popular young man with a penchant for puns, pilsner and games of chance. Later known worldwide as O. Henry, the short story writer got to reflect on the literary life for a while after being booked into the jail on a federal bank embezzlement rap in 1898.

Until 1923, under state law the sheriff of the county in which the condemned person had been convicted bore the responsibility of carrying out an execution. After that time, executions were by electrocution at the state prison in Huntsville.

For the superstitious, these are the other potential Greer Building "haints":

- Taylor Ake, eighteen, hanged August 22, 1879, for rape.
- Ed Nichols, twenty-one, hanged January 12, 1894, for rape.
- William Eugene Burt, hanged May 27, 1898, for killing his wife and two children. Police found their bodies dumped in a cistern at 207 East Ninth Street.
- Sam Watrus, thirty, hanged January 27, 1899, for murder, rape and robbery.
- Jim Davidson, thirty, hanged November 24, 1899, for murder, rape and robbery.
- Henry Williams, thirty, hanged May 2, 1904, for murder and rape.
- John Henry, hanged July 12, 1912, for murder.
- Henry Brook, hanged May 30, 1913, for murder.

While none of these men ever had to worry about the infirmities associated with the passage of time, by the late 1920s, the jail had begun to show its age. And so had the adjacent county courthouse at Eleventh and Congress. When Travis County officials decided to construct a new courthouse at Eleventh and Guadalupe Streets in 1930, the plans included a larger, state-of-the-art jail on the top floor of the new building.

The Highway Department, crammed in a state office building across the street from the old jail, saw the impending move as an opportunity to get land for a new headquarters. Negotiations soon began with Travis County to buy the property. "We wish to renew our recommendation that the State Highway Commission be permitted to erect a building to house the State Highway Department in Austin," read the fifth of nine recommendations made in the department's seventh biennial report. "Such a building," the 1930 report continued, should include "a laboratory, research department, and ample other space for carrying on its activities, now and in the future."

Despite the transportation agency's interest in the jail property, some Austinites suggested the old jail should be remodeled and transformed into a public library named in honor of O. Henry.

In the end, practicality trumped preservation, and the state razed the old jail. The department used free labor to clear the site, ordering a class of Highway Patrol cadets then in training at Camp Mabry to do the job.

At a cost of $455,151.74, the new building opened in the summer of 1933 only three years after it was requested. Impressive as the new Highway Building was, nearly another twenty years went by before the agency got around to installing air conditioning. That cost $170,642.00 in 1951.

The building has seen various renovations since then but no ghost busting.

CAPTAIN MERRILL'S CABIN

The old log cabin on the northern edge of Travis County amounts to an island of Texas past surrounded by Texas present.

Whoever built it knew that going to Austin for supplies meant a daylong wagon ride. For the most part, the family that called the cabin home fended for themselves when it came to acquiring food—or staying safe from hostile Indians.

More than 130 years went by before the city came to the cabin, a figurative brush fire of urbanization that threatened to obliterate not only the historic structure but also the way of life it represented. Fortunately, back in the early 1980s, men like Bill Todd, then maintenance supervisor for Provident Development—a Canadian-owned company planning a subdivision called Wells Branch—understood what would be lost if the cabin were bulldozed in the name of progress or even moved.

Working with developer Jim Mills and O.T. Baker, founder of the Institute of Texan Culture's Texas Folk Life Festival in San Antonio, Todd saved the old cabin. Today, as the rustic centerpiece of Katherine Fleischer Park, the cabin sits in the middle of a neighborhood with eight thousand residences occupied by twenty-thousand-plus people.

Todd missed being a native Texan by a day or two, but his Texas roots go deep. His parents were from Round Rock, but his father was in the army and

One of the oldest log cabins in Travis County, these days the old Gault family homestead is the centerpiece of Katherine Fleischer Park in far north Austin. *Photo by the author.*

the family moved from post to post. Todd was born in Toledo, Ohio, in 1920 while his father was en route to his latest assignment at Fort Sam Houston in San Antonio. Later, he followed his father's footsteps with a twenty-six-year army career. "Then I went to work for a living," he laughed. "I came back to Texas in 1977."

When Provident Development began buying land for Wells Branch in 1980, Todd joined the firm. The cabin, outhouse and rock smokehouse came with the nine-hundred-plus acres the company purchased for the subdivision. The fifteen- by fifteen-foot cabin had been built of artfully hewn cedar, one of the most durable of woods. Over the years, as its builder's family grew, so did the cabin. Other rooms were fashioned from milled lumber. Eventually, the cabin had four rooms, a long front porch and two stone fireplaces. "Fortunately, the roof held up," Todd said. "That's what saved this cabin. When a structure loses its roof, it's gone."

Even so, by the time Todd and others began restoring it, the old cabin definitely needed work. "I hauled off four loads of manure from inside,"

Todd recalled. "In fact, that's how I came to meet Baker. I took the manure to a riding stable off FM 1325 and ran into him. He asked what I was going to do with all that manure, and I said, 'Give it to you if you want it.'"

While Todd and his workers, with consultation from Baker, began transforming the old cabin into something like it must have looked in its prime, others started delving into its history.

The cabin may have been built in the late 1840s by Ohio-born Nelson Merrill, who settled on Brushy Creek in Williamson County in 1837. A couple years later, he headed a Ranger company that protected the Republic of Texas's new capital, a village named Austin. After statehood, Merrill moved in 1846 to Walnut Creek in Travis County. His land included the present site of the cabin, though no proof exists that he built it. A mile or so from the cabin, the former Ranger did start a community named in his honor, Merrilltown.

If Captain Merrill built the cabin, he did not have it long, selling the land in 1851 to J.P. Whelin. (Merrill eventually moved back to Williamson County, where he died in 1892.) Whelin held the property only a short time before conveying it to someone else. That owner, in turn, sold it to John M. Gault in 1853. His family kept the land for nearly forty years.

No matter who built it, the cabin has a good ghost story connected to it.

"When I first looked inside this cabin," Todd began, "it had no doors and was full of hay. In the corner of the original cabin, an old cow had fallen through the floor and died. It didn't even smell bad, mostly just bones."

Not long after the cabin's restoration, Todd happened to be sitting on the porch one day when he heard a funny noise. "The property was still being leased for cattle raising," Todd said. "I got up and looked around, but no cows."

Todd returned to what he was doing, which was making a pioneer-style broom for display at the cabin.

"Then I heard it again. Sounded like a little calf under the cabin." Again, Todd left his folk project to investigate. "I looked all around," he continued. "Maybe my eyes were going, but I still didn't see anything. But I definitely heard a cow or calf. Most old houses have people ghosts. I tell the kids that this cabin has cow ghosts."

TREASURE

THE OLD RANGER'S TREASURE MAP

When A.S. Lowery signed on with the Texas Rangers in 1875, the state paid its frontier lawmen thirty dollars a month. At some point during Lowery's half-year of service with famed Captain Leander H. McNeely, an old Mexican man came to him seeking help. His son had been stabbed to death, the man told the Ranger. If Lowery could catch the killer, the old man continued, he would make the lawman rich. Back in those days, peace officers routinely supplemented their pay with rewards offered for the arrest of wanted criminals. But the grieving father offered the Ranger another sort of incentive: a map leading to a hoard of lost silver.

The old man told the Ranger the treasure dated to 1825, when as a youth of thirteen his family and a few others came from the border to what is now Caldwell County (the closest community back then was Gonzales) to mine for silver. He said the second shaft they dug revealed a vein of silver ore near the Iron Mountains, a range of hills about nine miles northeast of present Luling.

The miners had produced forty-three bars of the precious metal when a rider informed them that hostile Indians had been seen in the area. Knowing they did not have enough manpower to defend themselves, the miners sealed the shaft with two large flat stones, covered them with smaller rocks and brush and then started packing to leave the area the following morning.

Unfortunately for the miners and their families, the Indians attacked their camp that night. All the men died, and the women and children were taken captive. He had been one of the captives, the "viejo" continued in his account to the state lawman. Eventually escaping from the Indians, he had settled near El Paso, where he married and raised a crop of children, including the son who got murdered.

Just how seriously Lowery took the old man is not known, but the Ranger's descendants later claimed he caught the killer. Lowery made the arrest when the man identified as the murderer crossed the Rio Grande into Texas near Del Rio to attend a Diaz y Seis celebration.

When he learned that the Ranger had apprehended his son's killer, who reportedly got life in prison for his crime, the old man looked up the lawman and handed him a crudely drawn map to the old mine. Lowery (state records show he served from June 22 to December 20, 1875) must not have put much stock in the document. His nephew, Harvey King, said in a 1937 newspaper interview that Lowery never made any effort to find the treasure. But in his dotage, the former Ranger got to thinking about the long-ago incident. In the early 1930s, King told his uncle that if he would give him the map, he would try to find the treasure. If he succeeded, he said, he would split it with him fifty-fifty.

"He refused," King told the reporter, "saying he would visit me in a few weeks and we would make the search [together]…but about the time he was to arrive I received a telegram he had died." The wire came on October 1, 1930.

King either got the map from someone else in the family or received an oral rundown on the vicinity of the supposed mine, because he visited the site in 1935. He later claimed he had no trouble finding a rock smelter and an old mine shaft that had been closed with dynamite. He saw signs that someone had been digging in the area but found nothing.

King died in 1951. Various people have tried to find the silver since then, but if anyone ever succeeded, no one talked.

While the story of the supposed Caldwell County silver mine is probably just another folk tale, there is one major difference in this one. Most treasure stories lack any physical evidence, save for the holes dug in search of supposed caches, but in this case, there are traces of the mine's existence. A newspaper reporter and photographer visiting the site back in the mid-1970s found a few pieces of slag, the waste product of a smelting operation.

A researcher who gained access to the site in 2002 documented what appeared to be a horizontal shaft called an adit and the remnants of an

L-shaped smelter constructed of cut sandstone. Someone using a metal detector found a few pieces of metal in the area but no silver bars.

The major problem with the site has to do with metallurgy. It would have taken tons of ore to produce forty-three bars of silver. All the slag from that would then have been near the smelter, but there was very little.

Even though it does not appear that any precious metal came out of the mine, no one has been able to determine the purpose of the smelter. Since some iron ore can be found in the area (hence the name Iron Mountains), it might have been an early-day ironworks. But again, where's all the slag?

Unless someone stumbles on the silver, the real treasure of Caldwell County can be found in nearby Lockhart—the barbecued brisket and sausage at Kreuz Market.

THE SWORD IN THE TREE

Way too high for anyone to reach, the hilt of a rusty sword protruded from the tree trunk near Walnut Creek in northern Travis County. "I saw it when I was in the seventh or eighth grade," says an Austin man now in his seventies who used to play along the creek in the late 1940s. "It looked like an old Spanish sword."

Obviously many years before, someone had left the weapon in the tree. Whether with a powerful slice the owner had wedged it into the side of the tree or thrust it through the whole tree when it was only a sapling, the tree had long since grown around the blade. And as the tree grew taller, the sword climbed higher.

The man who remembered seeing that mysterious sword—he doesn't want his real name used—related a tale of lost Spanish gold. Born in 1937 in a tent at a workers' camp during the construction of Lake Buchanan dam, the teller of this tale (call him Todd) later lived with his parents on ten acres off Middle Fiskville Road between Braker and Rundberg Lanes back when Austin's Lamar Boulevard also was the highway to Dallas. He and his friends played along Walnut Creek and its shorter tributary, Little Walnut Creek. They fished for bream, trapped raccoons for four bits a pelt and peppered anything that moved with their slingshots.

Todd's grandparents owned a business on East Avenue, which is where he met his friend Malcolm, who lived in the neighborhood. Malcolm had recently achieved some degree of local celebrity by winning a Schwinn bike in a yo-yo contest. Malcolm's uncle was Walter Stark, an Austin grocer who owned a place on Big Walnut Creek just to the east of the old Dallas highway only about four miles as the crow flies from where Todd lived. Though back then Stark's land lay well out in the country, the highway bridge over Lamar could be seen from his property.

That crossing is historic. For a short time, the Spanish operated a mission on the San Gabriel River, and future Lamar Boulevard would have been an old trail even then, likely blazed by buffalo and further worn by Indians. Spaniards operating out of San Antonio de Bexar well could have used that route, which connected low-water crossings from the Colorado River northward. Later, the government of the Republic of Texas called the trace the National Highway, and in the 1870s, it was a segment of the legendary Chisholm Trail.

The story Todd heard as a kid is classic folklore: A Spanish mule train laden with gold coins from Mexico was shadowed by Indians. Desperate to lighten their load and escape attack, the teamsters buried all the gold on the bank of a stream that would come to be called Walnut Creek. How the men had time to hide gold while trying to get away from hostile Indians is never explained. Of course, logic seldom gets in the way of a good treasure story.

To mark the spot, the tale continues, someone placed a sword in the tree, its blade pointing to the creek-side bluff into which a hole had been dug for the gold. And there the gold remained, or so the story goes.

Eventually Stark acquired the property and, at some point, bought in Mexico a map that purported to give the location of the loot. Based on this document, the landowner began an extensive excavation project. "He was sensitive about anyone being on his land, but his nephew and I sneaked on the place," Todd said. "Later we were able to get on it legitimately. Malcolm showed me the sword in the tree and some gold coins he said had been found along the creek. I also saw the tunnel that Stark had dug into the bluff. It was like a mine, on different levels. He even had tracks, electric lights and ore cars."

Todd finished the sixth grade at Fiskville School, went on to University Junior High in Austin and graduated from Austin High in 1954. He soon began a twenty-year U.S. Air Force career. Not long after he joined the military, his family sold their place on Middle Fiskville Road after learning it was about to be cut in half by a new highway to be called Interstate 35.

"If Stark ever found that gold on his place, I never heard about it," Todd says. "All I know is that I saw that old sword in the tree when I was a kid."

AN ANTIQUE WEAPONS CACHE SEALED IN CONCRETE?

The story sounded suspiciously like an urban legend, but the teller clearly believed it without question. It goes back to 1840, when Austin was capital of the Republic of Texas. The government had been there less than a year when an armory was built near the point where Waller Creek flowed into the Colorado River.

As Gerald Pierce said in his well-researched study of the republic's military, *Texas Under Arms*, no description of the arsenal is known. But, he speculated, it was "doubtless a small log and frame building much like the Houston Arsenal." The installation likely also had barracks, corrals, horse sheds and a blacksmith's shop.

The Austin armory also had a small shop where weapons could be repaired and tested. Machinery was powered by a water wheel in the nearby creek, which constituted the eastern edge of the frontier town. "Here was the real center of day-to-day army activity in…Austin," Pierce wrote, "and the only place in the town that was constantly occupied by Texan soldiers from 1839 to 1845."

Because of that, the creek and the few undeveloped spots around it at times attract modern-day metal detector enthusiasts who like to look for old buttons, buckles and bullets. And from one of them, a man who has been listening to the whine of a radio signal bouncing up from buried metal for more than three decades, comes this story. "When they were excavating for a new building at the site several years ago," he said, "the workmen found a tunnel underneath where the arsenal had stood." That is interesting enough, but what he said next borders on the incredible: "Inside the tunnel were stacks of rifles and swords."

When the heavy equipment crew reported the find to the contractor, his reaction was not one of historical fascination, the metal detector said. "Fill it up with concrete," the boss man supposedly ordered.

The contractor feared that if he reported the find, the project would be delayed by archaeologists and all the associated governmental red tape. So, on penalty of losing their job, the workmen poured concrete into the tunnel.

Supposedly, the weapons were left inside so word would not get out, but that's pretty hard to swallow. How could anyone resist getting their hands on a vintage firearm or sword?

If there really is a historical treasure-trove beneath downtown Austin, maybe the next time someone gets the site ready for a new building, someone will wonder about an unusual, tunnel-shaped core of buried concrete.

More likely, it's just a legend.

GETTING THERE AND BACK

THE NIGHT THE BEER TRAIN WRECKED

Hamilton Wright expected a quiet evening. In his experience, almost all nights passed that way. But things were about to come to a head, so to speak.

Working the night telegrapher's shift at the Buda train depot south of Austin, around 11:00 p.m. Wright got word over the wire that a freight train bound from San Antonio to Austin had derailed on a curve of track at the entrance of the Bear Creek railroad bridge just south of the Capital City. Hamilton had heard the north-bound train rumble through the small Hays County town only a few minutes before the accident.

The engine and its tender had jumped the track, which in turn caused the freight cars to plummet off the bridge into the dry creek below. The engineer and the fireman both lay dead in the wreckage.

From his post eight miles south of the scene, Wright listened as the wire came alive. The train dispatcher in San Antonio ordered a wrecker to proceed from Taylor, the railroad's division point, to the location of the derailment. In addition, the telegraph directed, all section foremen needed to gather gandy dancers—railroad slang for track workers—to join the work train headed to the wreck site. The foreman in Austin received instructions to "gather everybody that would work" on Congress Avenue and hire them for the duration of the emergency.

A wreck blocking the mainline between Austin and San Antonio was serious enough, but this derailment posed even worse problems. Not only

Both the engineer and fireman died, but that didn't slack the thirst of those who rushed to the scene of the train accident. *Author's collection.*

had there been two casualties, but the accident had also occurred at a point where temporary trackage could not be laid to divert passenger trains and other freights. On top of that, Wright knew that the refrigerated cars telescoped on each other held a liquid cargo capable of causing other issues. As railroad officials and local authorities soon found out, while not explosive or toxic, a spilled trainload of beer could be problematic, to say the least.

Known simply as "the beer train," this particular run left the Alamo City every night laden with newly bottled beer from the Pearl and Lone Star Breweries. It also carried a heavy cargo of beer in stout wooden barrels, all bound for the flourishing saloons in the Capital City and points northeast along the line. "Barrels rolled out and cases of bottled beer tumbled here and there, some bottles breaking but other lying invitingly to anyone near," Wright later recalled.

Before long, word leaked out along with some of the beer that free-for-the-taking containers of the best of the brewers' craft lay scattered around the yet unguarded train wreck. While the railroad desperately tried to recruit men willing to work hard and long for $1.25 a day, others more than happy to expend a little effort in harvesting hops—well, the liquid product derived from the grain—saddled their horses or raced their buggies to the scene of the wreck.

When the railroad work train reached the wreck at 2:00 a.m., railroadmen and the newly hired workers found a rescue party already on hand, "party" being the operative word. Numerous barrels had been rolled off and tapped, revelers having a literal free (beer) for all, with no peace officers having arrived to spoil the fun.

And it soon got worse, at least from the railroad's perspective. Many of its newly hired gandy dancers gave up their jobs on the spot, figuring they could easily drink or steal for later consumption more than $1.25 worth of beer in less time than it would take to earn the same amount in cash with hard work. As the crowd's collective blood alcohol level began to rise with the decline in the beer supply, fights started breaking out. "In a few hours," Wright recalled, "the gulches and level places within a half mile of the wreck looked like a Baccanalia outrivaling anything Rome ever attempted."

With beer-breathed drunks everywhere, some of them already sick from overindulgence, some still quaffing the "free" booze and others sprawled on the ground battered and bloody from fighting, anyone newly arrived to the scene must have thought a true human disaster had occurred.

Finally, Travis County sheriff's deputies, hastily deputized area citizens and even Austin police officers arrived. Twisting arms and swinging billy clubs, they began making arrests and slowly restored order. By the time this second, figurative train wreck had been cleaned up, some two hundred men had been hauled off to the hoosegow.

Working around the clock, the railroad crews had the wreckage cleared and the tracks reopened within forty-eight hours. While the beer could not be salvaged, those barrels that remained intact were returned to the breweries for reuse. For decades after the incident, Wright said, the area around the wreck site was covered with empty or broken beer bottles.

AN EIGHTEEN-MILE-LONG MUD HOLE

Motorists today tend to take good roads for granted, unless they encounter bumpy pavement, a detour or congested traffic. But in the early twentieth century, travelers well understood the old expression that compared something unfavorable to "X miles of bad road."

When J.D. Copeland hired on as a rural mail carrier in Travis County in 1916, he quickly learned the importance of good roads. Using a gig, a two-wheeled wagon pulled by one horse, Copeland served a twenty-four-and-a-half-mile route in the southeastern part of the county, working out of the Del Valle Post Office. Of that route, only six miles of road had a gravel covering. The rest of the mileage consisted of two-rut dirt roads.

"During rainy weather I had just one mud hole about eighteen miles long between two barbed wire fences," Copeland later recalled. Noting that on occasion a wet spell could last up to six weeks, he continued, "I had to go horse back, carrying four pouches of mail hanging two on each side of the horse, over the front and back of the saddle."

When making his deliveries on a horse, he carried only first-class mail, daily newspapers and magazines. He saved the catalogs and parcels until the weather—and the roads—improved.

Copeland never forgot a particularly wet spring that washed out bridges as well as making the roads virtually impassable. Conditions one day deteriorated to the point that he had to switch from a horse to a mule. When he tried to ford Dry Creek, a name that seemed like a joke at the time, his mule decided to lie down in the cool mud at the creek's edge. Copeland soon found himself mired in silt and water up to his waist. "At that time I told myself I was quitting," he said.

Copeland managed to make it to a country store in the nearby Stony Point community. There, the proprietor loaned him a change of clothes and agreed to hold his mail until Copeland's customers could come and claim it.

Back at Del Valle, Copeland walked in the post office and advised Postmaster James H. Johnson that he needed to find a new carrier for his route. "I told [Johnson] that I was quitting for the reason that only a jaybird could fly over those mud holes," Copeland said. "He laughed and told me to go home and he would study about sending my resignation in the next morning."

After sleeping on it, Copeland returned to the post office for another talk with Johnson. The young mailman may or may not have heard the often-invoked expression first articulated by the Greek historian Herodotus that "Neither snow, nor rain, nor heat, nor gloom of nights, stays these couriers from the swift completion of their appointed rounds," but he knew the fundamentals of microeconomics: it takes money to pay the rent and buy food.

"I had dried out and thawed out [and told] the postmaster that I had a wife and two children that I had to provide for and I'd try a while longer," Copeland said.

Postmaster Johnson stayed on the job a while longer himself, finally retiring in the summer of 1946 after thirty-four years on the job. That was about when the highway department started building an all-weather network of paved rural routes called farm to market roads that made it a lot easier for postal carriers to live up to Herodotus's words.

Laughing Matters

The Mayor Ordered a Wedding

She possessed a lyrically evocative name few would believe, a life few would envy. Her name was Belle Christmas. Nearly a century after figuring in a tale Charles Dickens surely would have fancied, how she came by her festive-sounding handle can only be a matter of speculation. Perhaps Belle's birthday fell on December 25. Maybe her parents simply liked the two words. Another possibility is that she was a damsel of the demimonde and took it as her professional name. No matter how she came to be called Belle Christmas, she had a reputation as a local character.

In the early 1900s, decades before construction of the dam that created Lady Bird Lake (originally Town Lake), the area of the Capital City between West First Street and the Colorado River was a squalid neighborhood of shacks on the edge of the red-light district, which began at Second Street.

As a young newspaperman, Edmunds Travis covered this rough side of Austin, as well as other goings-on, often riding to the scene of a shooting or stabbing on the back of a policeman's horse. Eventually becoming a newspaper editor and still later a highly influential lobbyist, Travis recalled the story of Belle Christmas in 1970.

Puffing on his pipe, he began the story with the necessary background. Many of those who lived in the shanties along the river made meager livings as commercial fishermen. Conservation laws prohibiting the taking of freshwater game fish for sale had not yet been passed, and even if it had been

As a young newspaperman, Edmunds Travis covered the sad story of Belle Christmas. *Author's collection.*

against the law, the fishermen would have gotten around it somehow. They could have cared less as long as they could land bass and catfish.

While some of them may have been hardworking family men just trying to get by, the majority of this class, according to Travis, "either drank or ate cocaine leaves…they were cocaine fiends." They would sell their catch to Austin restaurants or markets only to use most of the proceeds to support their drug habits. When the last of their drug supply wore off, they went back to work.

One of those "louts," as Travis called them, had a girlfriend—Belle Christmas. While the couple apparently got along well enough when he was sober, one day he got high, turned mean and practically beat her to death. The police arrested him and hauled him off as Belle sobbed.

Despite the injuries he had inflicted on her, Belle soon came to see him at the city jail, which occupied the basement of city hall. Whether she had intended to get her boyfriend out of the clink is not known, but the opportunity presented itself when the officer who let her in forgot to lock the door. Belle sprang her lover, and they hurried back to their riverbank abode.

But Austin was a small town. It did not take the authorities long to locate the escaped fishmonger. And this time, they arrested Belle for her role in his getaway.

Back then, the mayor also presided over recorder's court, the equivalent of today's municipal court—a legal entity with jurisdiction only over misdemeanor cases. The mayor was Alexander Penn Wooldridge, who served from 1909 to 1919. A compassionate man who believed in the importance of education and public parks, Wooldridge found it touching that Belle would free the very man who had roughed her up so badly. At the same time, he viewed their cohabitation as morally reprehensible

In relating this story, Travis did not give the season of its occurrence. But it must have been around the holiday for which Belle had been named, a time of year when many people get the urge to make things better for the less fortunate. Wooldridge had no immunity from such feelings. Summoning the couple to his office, the mayor lectured the man not only for having hurt Belle but also for doing her wrong. In fact, Wooldridge said, he "ought to be ashamed for dragging Belle into the gutter." To make it right, the mayor continued, the man needed to marry Belle.

"I don't think so," the fisherman said defiantly.

"Well," Wooldridge countered, "I'll keep you in jail until you do."

Mentally weighing the invisible shackles of marriage against actual confinement behind bars, the man caved in. Being as how the mayor thought it proper, he would gladly take Belle's hand in marriage. If a look of doubt momentarily clouded Belle's bruised face, the mayor did not pick up on it. Forgoing the formalities of a license, Wooldridge pronounced them man and wife right there and cheerfully bade them good luck and many years of marital bliss.

A week later, a sober but noticeably agitated Mr. Belle Christmas showed up at city hall and demanded an audience with the mayor. "You got me in trouble and now you've got to get me out of it," he said. "Belle's husband is really raising hell about this marriage."

According to Travis, the embarrassed mayor ordered the couple to separate and seek a divorce. Apparently, he opted to take no judicial notice of Belle Christmas's accidental descent into bigamy.

What became of Belle after that has not been determined, but Mayor Wooldridge probably proceeded somewhat more cautiously the next time he got the urge to do a little matchmaking.

THE RIFLE WITH THE BENT BARREL

Maybe someday a scuba diver will find the old bent rifle barrel at the bottom of Lake Travis. It's bound to be there somewhere, resting in the sediment in the vicinity of Hudson Bend.

When Wiley Hudson came to Travis County in 1854, settling above Austin in a bend of the Colorado River that came to bear his family's name, no one would have considered doing so without a good rifle close at hand. The state capital lay a day's wagon ride downstream, but hostile Indians still posed a threat in the area.

Six years after Hudson built his cabin on the river west of Austin, a federal census enumerator listed Hudson and his wife, Catherine, as having eight children. Hudson's father and two brothers also lived along the bend. All of the Hudson clan got by as farmer-ranchers, though when the Civil War broke out, the Hudson boys shouldered arms for the Confederacy. After the war, the Hudsons returned to the Colorado, enduring droughts and floods as they made their living off the land.

On almost any farm in early-day Texas, corn figured as an important crop. The Hudsons and their fellow settlers carried the corn by wagon to Anderson Mill, where the yellow kernels could be ground into meal and eventually transformed into corn bread.

By the time Hudson had grandchildren, the families living in the cedar-covered hills west of Austin no longer feared raiding Comanches. But

The Hudsons used to get their corn ground at nearby Anderson's Mill. *Photo by the author.*

well into the twentieth century, a rifle still hung above every mantel. And a Texan learned how to shoot early.

One day in the 1930s, one of the Hudson grandsons busied himself plunking a single-shot .22 around his family's riverside homestead. Wearying of the hornet's buzz of speeding bullets, the grandpa told the boy to be careful where he aimed. He especially cautioned him against shooting around the mules. The animals, hitched to a wagon full of corn, had a deserved reputation for skittishness. But boys being boys, the youngster kept the lead flying. When a bullet whistled past the long ear of one of Hudson's mules, both animals jumped straight into the air and came down going in opposite directions.

Recovering enough to pull together, the mules ran wildly, pulling the corn-laden wagon behind them. The team ran through a gate, catching the wagon behind them. That broke the gate and wrecked the wagon, covering the ground with mounds of corn.

Seeing the semi-disastrous consequences of his disregarded warning, the elder Hudson flew out of the house in pursuit of his errant grandson. Grabbing the bolt-action rifle from the boy, the old man smashed it into the closest pecan, wrapping the barrel around the sturdy tree. Unreconstructed, the young man picked up the .22 and smarted off: "Now I can shoot around corners!"

At that, Hudson retrieved the rifle and hurled it out into the river.

A few years later, the newly created Lower Colorado River Authority began buying land along the river in anticipation of building a large flood control dam. With the completion of Mansfield Dam in 1940 and the filling of Lake Travis, about half the original Hudson acreage flooded. Remains were exhumed from the old family cemetery and relocated at Teck, just off present Ranch Road 620.

The area around the new community of Hudson Bend has boomed, with subdivisions and expensive homes covering much of the old farm and ranch land. And somewhere out there in the lake is a rifle barrel with a story.

The Banker and the Lightning Rod Salesman

The farmer climbed in his old pickup and drove into Taylor to see his banker. His usual cigar clamped firmly in his mouth, the banker cordially invited his longtime customer to sit down and tell him how he could be of service.

"Well, I need to borrow a couple of thousand dollars," the farmer said.

"What for?" the banker asked, gumming his stogie. "You had a good cotton crop this year. Everybody around here did."

"Something unexpected came up," he farmer said. "A lightning rod salesman came by the other day and told me my barn was an accident waiting to happen. One bolt of lightning and it'd burn down. I can't afford to lose my barn."

The banker bit down a little harder on his soggy cigar.

"You can't afford to buy $2,000 worth of lightning rods, either," he said. "In the first place, I don't think lightning rods work. In the second place, $2,000 is too damn much money for two or three pieces of metal and some fancy glass bulbs. I'm not loaning you the money."

Unable to finance the purchase, the farmer turned down the lightning rod man. Shrugging, the salesman moved on. Texas had no shortage of suckers. The traveling salesman who lost a deal in Williamson County on account of a frugal country banker practiced a not-so-honorable trade dating back to the 1700s.

In 1749, Benjamin Franklin became the first scientist to opine that lightning rods could protect buildings, churches, houses and barns from thunderstorm-generated electrical discharges, better known as lightning bolts. As soon as lightning rods entered into commercial production, peddlers of protection began steepling America with the ornate iron rods. If nothing else, the score or more of lightning dissipation devices patented since the mid-eighteenth century at least served one purpose—they made people feel safer.

No one doubted the power of a fifty-thousand-degree, billon-volt bolt from above. Well into the 1930s, people in and around the Dallas County town of Wilmer still talked about a fierce thunderstorm that hit the community

Traveling salesmen peddled lightning rods and a false sense of security. *Author's collection.*

on August 10, 1897, when rain and lightning forced a wheat-thrashing crew to seek shelter in a newly built barn. But lightning struck the roof, killing a man and his eight-year-old son, as well as another member of the work crew. A horse and a mule also died from the blast from above. When the barn and adjacent farmhouse went on the market a few years later, charred pieces of clothing still stuck to a portion of its interior wall. The new owner immediately had lightning rods installed.

But by the early 1950s, the popularity of lightning rods had waned substantially. Old lightning rods became collectibles and are about as easy to find these days as a locally owned bank or a banker like the one who nixed his valued customer's oral application for a lightning rod loan.

Retired Texas National Guard public information officer Ed Komandosky of Taylor later had the same banker. For a time, he even worked for him. "Money is for having," Komandosky said the banker used to tell him, "not spending."

That must have been why the banker once refused to sign a note so Komandosky could buy a new car. "You don't need a new car," the banker told him. "The one you've got is just fine." In fact, the car the banker owned had rolled off the assembly line years before the "old" vehicle Komandosky wanted to replace with a newer ride.

Of course, the Taylor bank president didn't turn down every loan application made at his bank. If he had done that, his institution would not have had much money to loan. But he was judicious in putting his name on someone's note. According to Komandosky, the banker's more savvy customers watched his cigar to judge how they were doing in making their case for a loan. "He always kept his cigar on the right side of his mouth," Komandosky remembered. "But if he decided to sign someone's note, he'd move that cigar to the left side." If the banker kept his cigar firmly in place on the right side of his mouth, his loan applicants knew they had to keep talking.

By the time the banker approved his last note, cigar smoking had declined sharply, and lightning rod salesmen had gone the way of most other door-to-door marketers. And recent research tends to back up the longtime Taylor banker's belief that lightning rods don't work.

The National Fire Protection Association (NFPA) first developed standards for lightning rods in 1904. NFPA codes are not law, but they have been adopted into the fire codes of most local governments. In the 1990s, the association came under pressure to modernize the part of its suggested code dealing with lightning rods, which in setting standards for their placement in effect endorsed such devices as scientifically proven to prevent lightning strikes.

Now, as the online encyclopedia Wikipedia says, "No major standards body, such as the NFPA…has currently endorsed a device that can prevent or reduce lighting strikes."

Traditions

Rock Fences

From Boerne to Burnet and beyond, the Hill Country is noted for its numerous rock fences, stock pens and cemetery enclosures. You see these fences most often in counties settled by German immigrants, but a more fundamental common denominator is the availability of building material—variably shaped rocks. Far more lasting than wooden rail fences, this type of enclosure was common before the advent of barbed wire, though some of them were built as late as the early 1900s. Most of them still stand more than a century and a half after being built.

Louis Grosz, born in Hueffenhardt, Germany, in 1853, came to Texas when he was eighteen. His uncle, Phillipp Eckert of Mason County, had written and told him what tools he needed to bring to make a living in America. Grosz weighed his two trunks down with iron, including a broad axe needed to build a log cabin.

As Estella Hartmann Orrison related in a family history she self-published in 1957, *Eckert Record*, when Grosz finally reached the Hill Country, he had to go to work to repay the fifty dollars his uncle had advanced him for his passage to Texas. His first income came from laying rock fences at fifty cents a day in an era decades before anyone had considered working only eight hours out of twenty-four.

Toiling from can see to can't, Grosz's rate of compensation amounted to only pennies on the hour. And the work must have been brutally hard. Roy

Many old rock fences like this still stand in Central Texas. *Photo by the author.*

Bedichek, in his 1947 book *Adventures with a Texas Naturalist*, estimated the stone fences on his place in Hays County weighed "not less than a ton per linear yard." The rule of thumb passed down to the present is that it took one man one day to build three feet of fence three feet high.

That three-feet-a-day pace involved not only the relatively mindless toil of finding, digging up, lifting and hauling suitable rocks but also the more cerebral activity of sorting and stacking them just so. Gravity held these fences together, not mortar. The rocks had to fit snugly and be balanced just right. Picture working a gigantic puzzle with very heavy pieces in a climate where most of the time it's too hot and sometimes too wet or cold or both. Throw in a sore back and the occasional displaced scorpion or rattlesnake, and you have a pretty tough way to make four bits a day. Oh, and hostile Indians still posed a danger in Mason County when Grosz had to earn money as a rock fence builder.

While rock fences also are known as "German fences," research by University of Texas graduate Laura Knott, a landscape architect specializing in historic preservation, revealed that dry-laid fences did not originate in Germany. Rather, the style used in Texas and elsewhere in the South seems to have been modeled after rock fences common to Great Britain. Knott theorized that German Texans learned of the style and imitated it. On the other hand, it doesn't take a rock-it scientist to figure that a potential farm field strewn with plow-breaking stones could be both fenced and cleared by stacking those very stones.

Their origin aside, rock fences are of two varieties: single-thickness walls about one foot wide and double-sided structures. Those two-siders, obviously, stood the stoutest. In building the thicker fences, a rock-stacking artisan put up one wall and then another parallel to it, leaving enough room in between for a fill of smaller stones called "hearting." The builder connected the two walls with long, flat stones known as "throughs."

In the course of her university research, Knott found a Blanco County farmer named John Cox (no relation to author) who learned both fence building and some philosophy from his father. "I remember a day that he was building fences and I was learning," Knott quoted Cox. "'Rocks must fit as close as words,' he said as he put a rock in place...He never put a stone where it didn't want to stay. 'Work with nature, not against it...if you want a fence to stand.'"

As for Grosz, after repaying his relative by laboring at fence building, he moved on to easier ways of making money like blacksmithing, furniture building, stone cutting and farming. In between, he and his wife raised eleven children.

Though Grosz could do many things, he must have been pretty handy at the work that paid for his immigration. He continued to hire out periodically as a fence builder. When his sons had grown strong enough, he put them to work hauling rocks while he did the exacting stacking that required more experience. He continued to build stone fences even after wire made them obsolete.

Like railroad workers laying track, the Groszes stayed in the field until they finished a job, moving their campsite as their enduring handiwork slowly progressed across a field. Twice a week, Grosz would send his boys home to fetch more grub while he stayed in camp near the fence in progress.

A relapse of measles, not hard work, killed Grosz at the age of forty-five in the spring of 1899. They buried him in the Gooch Cemetery on the eastern edge of Mason. Most, if not all, of his rock fences still stand.

CROGHAN COBBLER

Texas has thousands of ancient oaks and other varieties of trees that have been around for a long time, but peach trees are a different story. More formally known as *Prunus persica*, peach trees are not indigenous to the Lone Star State. They are believed to have originated in China, migrating from there along the trade routes to Persia (Iran) and from the Middle East to North Africa and Europe. As America began to be colonized, Europeans brought peach seedlings with them.

Though peaches are found around the world, they nevertheless are picky about where they will grow. They do best in sandy soil and need at least three weeks of cold weather to be able to flower and produce fruit.

The commercial hot spots in Texas, which ranks ninth in the nation in production of peaches, are the Hill Country, particularly Gillespie and surrounding counties, East Texas around Smith County and North Texas, centered in Montague and adjoining counties. The Central Texas town of Stonewall calls itself the Peach Capital of Texas. The four thousand or so acres of peach trees in the Hill Country produce about a third of the state's peach crop each year.

Wherever they grow, if a peach tree makes it to the ripe old age of thirty, it has lived an unusually long life. Indeed, most peach trees seldom make it past their first decade of existence. That's what made the peach tree outside the old stone structure in Burnet at the site of Fort Croghan so unusual. No one could remember how long it had stood there, but every summer, it still bore tasty if somewhat tart peaches.

This stone structure served as the powder house at Fort Croghan. Years later, a nearby peach tree for a time provided the local historical society with cobbler every summer. *Author's collection.*

The U.S. Army's Second Dragoons established the fort in 1849 to protect the area from hostile Indians. After the military abandoned the post overlooking Hamilton Creek in 1853, settlers moved into some of the old government structures, including the small rock building where the peach tree still flourished in the early 1960s.

Some said whoever had lived there must have planted the tree. Others said its proximity to the entrance of the structure indicated someone might simply have discarded a moist peach seed that took root and flourished on its own. However it came to be at Fort Croghan, the fruit tree had been there a good while.

I first saw the tree, and tasted its fruit, in the summer of 1963. A precocious teenager as interested in Texas history as girls and cars, I attended (thanks to my late mother, who drove me there) that year's annual meeting of the Burnet County Historical Society. After duly handling their old and new business, members and guests enjoyed a potluck picnic topped off with a cobbler made by Mrs. L.C. Ross with peaches from the tree that grew at the fort.

Mrs. Ross had been president of the society in 1960, the year the group began working to restore the old fort. While at the site that year, she told me later, she picked the choicest peaches from the tree "before the squirrels and birds got to them." She baked them in a cobbler for the society's annual meeting, and a tradition had begun.

The longevity of that Fort Croghan peach tree is all the more unusual considering the care a peach tree normally requires. It has to be pruned after the first hard freeze in the fall, a process that must continue through early spring when the trees bloom. Since the trees normally produce more fruit than they can ripen, they have to been thinned of fruit to keep peaches spaced six to eight inches apart. Too, a peach tree takes a lot of water and weeding. It also needs to be protected from insects and plant diseases.

Another venerable peach tree once grew in Lampasas County. In the early 1930s, a tree belonging to L.W. McCrea measured six feet in circumference. At the time (1934), it was considered one of the oldest peach trees in Texas. McCrea said his family planted the tree in the late 1860s or early 1870s.

A few years after enjoying my first Croghan cobbler, I was with my granddad when he stopped to buy some peaches at a roadside stand between Fredericksburg and Stonewall. When we walked in the tent, two women about my granddad's age sat happily gossiping away in German. As Granddad selected a basket of peaches, they continued their conversation, secure in their belief that the older man and teenage boy—obviously tourists—knew nothing of the language they spoke.

What they did not know was that my granddad's last name was Wilke. His grandfather, Herman Wilke, had settled in Fredericksburg in 1850. Granddad grew up hearing German spoken and, all those years later, still knew a little of his ancestral tongue.

As we walked away, the women resumed their German discussion. Suddenly, acting as if he'd almost forgotten his manners, Granddad stopped and turned toward the two gossips. "*Danke schoen,*" he said with a smile. Realizing he must have understood what they had been talking about, the women froze worse than a peach orchard hit by a late March norther.

Here's Mrs. Ross's Croghan cobbler recipe:

Boil a quart of peeled and cut peaches until tender. Add:
1½ cups sugar
1 tablespoon cinnamon
½ tablespoon nutmeg
½ stick butter or margarine

Crust:
½ cup water
⅞ cup lard or oil
pinch of salt and enough flour to make stiff dough

Roll out on floured board, cut dough in strips and lay over half the
fruit in a shallow baking dish or pan. Add the rest of the peaches
and another layer of dough.
Bake at 425 degrees until bubbly with a brown crust.

MEMORIES OF CHRISTMAS PAST:
GINGERBREAD AND GUNFIRE

Christmas in Central Texas back during what came to be called "the panic
of '06" wasn't the jolliest of times. My late granddad used to tell me about
a decidedly Dickensian Christmas Eve in 1906. Money was tight, and as the
oldest of five kids, my grandfather did not expect to get much of anything
for Christmas.

But sometime that evening, his father left their modest house on what was
then the northern edge of Austin. The son of an early Fredericksburg settler,
it was my great-grandfather Adolph Wilke's habit to drop by Scholtz's Beer
Garden on San Jacinto Street in the evening and buy some sausage and a
bucket of beer to go. The term "to go," of course, had not yet been coined.
And health laws have long since precluded selling beer by the bucket.

When he got home, however, Wilke was not toting beer or sausage.
Instead, he carefully carried a lard can lid nearly as big as a wagon wheel.
Inside his family's small frame house, he presented the children with a
family-size gingerbread boy, fresh from the Lundquest Bakery on Congress
Avenue. The bakery had either given or loaned him that lard can lid to
keep the fresh-out-of-the-oven pastry intact until the kids could tear into it.
As Granddad later told it, when he and his sisters and little brother lit into
that hot gingerbread, they thought they were having a pretty fine Christmas
despite the nation's financial slump.

More than a half century later, my mother struggled to come up with
a gift idea for her father, who was, at that stage of his career, a "man who
has everything." At some point, she remembered Granddad's story of the
Christmas gingerbread boy and decided to make it happen for him again.

A big gingerbread boy from Austin's Lundberg Bakery brightened a family's Christmas in 1906. *Author's collection.*

Letting her fingers do the walking, she located a business firm willing to give her a metal barrel lid roughly equivalent to the king-sized lard can top my granddad remembered from that long-ago holiday. Then Mother baked a Texas-size gingerbread boy and delivered it to Granddad atop that lid.

Many Texas families have their particular Christmas traditions, but the way the Hornsby clan used to observe the holiday may just take the fruitcake. Reuben Hornsby, born in Georgia and raised in Mississippi, came to Texas in the early summer of 1830. Soon he obtained a one-labor headright from Stephen F. Austin for land in the impresario's newly organized upper colony, which extended up the Colorado River.

Hornsby built a log cabin on the land in 1832 and received full title to it nine years later. Located on the east bank of the Colorado thirty miles north of Bastrop in what is now Travis County, his land and the settlement that began there came to be called Hornsby Bend.

"A more beautiful tract of land," historian John W. Wilbarger later wrote, "can nowhere be found than the league of land granted to Reuben Hornsby. Washed on the west by the Colorado, it stretches over a level valley about three miles wide to the east, and was…covered with wild rye, and looking like one vast green wheat field."

The land was fruitful, and so were Hornsby and his wife, Sarah. They had ten children, the seed stock of one of Texas's oldest and best-known extended families.

Being on the far edge of what passed for civilization in early Texas, Hornsby and his family had a lot of trouble with Indians. Hornsby rode as a Texas Ranger and had several scrapes with the Comanches. In fact, Indians snuck up on his son Daniel Hornsby and a friend in 1845 while they fished in the river and killed them both.

Reuben lived on for another third of a century, dying on January 11, 1879. His family and friends buried him in the Hornsby Bend Cemetery next to his wife, who had preceded him in death by seventeen years.

By that time, Hornsbys lived all along the river below Austin. One of those Hornsbys was Reuben Addison Hornsby, whom the family credits with starting the tradition of letting loose with a blast from his shotgun every Christmas morning. But it was not just a one-volley salute. As soon as Reuben Addison fired his scatter gun, neighbor Jess Hornsby would pull the trigger on his shotgun. That shot would, in turn, be answered by a round from neighbor Mark Gilbert, followed by shots from Smith Hornsby and Spurge Parsons. Wallace Hornsby, who lived up the road, fired next, usually touching off two shots. The sound of gunfire continued to echo along the river as Ernest Robertson and Jim Hornsby joined in on the annual yuletide salute.

One year, according to Hornsby family lore, neighbor Tett Cox had not had enough coffee before shouldering his shotgun. He dropped the hammer too close to his front porch, accidentally blowing a hole in his roof. Still, the holiday morning fusillade went on. It was the way they said Merry Christmas to each other. August Foster fired next, followed by Paul Rowe, who lived near the Hornsby burial ground, and then Vince McLaurin. From farther downstream came shots fired by Malcolm Hornsby, Willie Platt, Jimmie Platt and Sam Platt. But just to be different, Sam Platt used his .45 revolver in welcoming Christmas Day.

The years went by, and the shooters began marrying and moving off or dying. Slowly, the tradition faded like dissipating gun smoke.

One Christmas morning, Harry Hornsby grabbed his shotgun, stepped outside and filled the cold morning air with the sound of a shot. He stood waiting for an answer, but none came. For all anyone living in the area knew, someone had taken a shot at a turkey or was showing their son how to fire the shotgun he'd gotten for Christmas.

Walking inside, Hornsby put the weapon away with the realization that he was the last member of the family who remembered the old tradition. It was the last shotgun Merry Christmas heard along Hornsby Bend.

NEW YEAR'S EVE IN STRING PRAIRIE

"You boys drink beer?" the old man asked, his German accent heavy on that last word. "I'm buyin'."

The oldest of the three men had just lost his younger brother to lung cancer. One of the "boys" was the recently departed's son, the other the dead man's son-in-law.

Having accomplished their mission of buying some eggs needed for the traditional post-passing family feed, enjoying a cold one or two didn't seem like a bad idea on an otherwise bleak winter day. When they pulled into a Bastrop convenience store, the old man got out of the car and hobbled in to get a couple of six-packs.

"I'm sho glad to get out of the house for a while," the benefactor said when he got back in the vehicle, popping a top. He sat in the back seat, resting his beer can on the knee of his artificial leg so the cold wouldn't bother him.

"This April, it'll be fifty years since I've had this damn thing," he said, tapping his leg with the bottom of his beer. "I was working at the rock quarry in New Braunfels, and it wouldn't have happened if I'd gotten off a damn hour earlier. I was supposed to get off at 3:00 a.m., and it happened right before 2:00." He swallowed some more beer and didn't finish the story. What happened was a railroad car had been backed up to take on a load of stone and he didn't get out of the way in time.

Losing a leg slowed him down, but it hadn't atrophied the pleasure he took in having a good time or telling a good tale. Like the time he nearly lost more than his leg during a once-annual event folks in Bastrop County referred to as the New Year's Shooting. While the end-of-the-year celebration did involve the discharge of firearms, it wasn't a "shooting" in the sense of hostile shots being fired. Well, there was one time.

Back in 1917, the small Bastrop County community of String Prairie had a group of about fifteen teenage boys old enough to have acquired a taste for the homemade Mustang grape wine their German American fathers put up every year but not quite old enough to worry about the terrible war going on in Europe. About 10:00 p.m. on that long-ago New Year's Eve, the boys saddled their horses and rode to a central meeting point. As soon as they felt they had a quorum, they started riding from farm to farm, ringing bells and shooting fireworks and, occasionally, the shotguns two of the older boys carried across their saddles. One of those older boys toting a scatter gun was the now elderly fellow telling the story between sips of beer.

The String Prairie boys made a fearsome-looking outfit, the old man recalled. Old-timers in the county hadn't seen anything like it since Reconstruction, when the governor had to call in the militia to quiet things down in nearby Cedar Creek because a more malevolent band of night riders seemed to be having trouble remembering the Civil War was over and their side had lost.

With the later-day teller of the tale in the lead, the boys trotted from farmhouse to farmhouse. When they arrived, they ringed the house with their horses and proceeded to make as much racket as they could in celebration of the New Year. Local custom held that when the boys showed up, the residents would listen for a while and then step out on their porch to invite the celebrants in for one glass of wine and one cookie. The riders would then thank the host, wish them a happy and prosperous New Year and mount up to ride off to the next rural residence.

Full of holiday cheer and homemade wine, the young horsemen of A-Cup-to-Their-Lips surrounded the next house on their circuit only to find all the lamps were out. But they knew the family was home because their buggy was in the barn. As they had done at all the previous stops that night, the riders rang their bells, set off firecrackers and generally made as much noise as fifteen tipsy teenage boys on the verge of manhood could make. Still, the house remained dark, its occupants obviously not in a social mood.

That's when the narrator of the tale said he decided to let loose with a double-barrel load of birdshot in the general direction of the house. Having no intention of hurting anyone, his only interest lay in getting their attention and another glass of wine.

And it worked—sort of. As the boys continued to whoop and holler, no one noticed the octagonal barrel of an old .30-30 slowly emerging from a quietly opened front door. Their first indication that their presence had been noted was a sudden blaze of orange flame as a hunk of lead whizzed by within a few inches of the narrator's head.

Clearly, the man of the house had no interest in sharing wine and cookies with a bunch of boozy kids ill mannered enough to ignore the fact that he'd blacked out his house. While the boys may have let their horses run a little between houses earlier in the evening, their mass retreat looked something like a reverse cavalry charge as they scattered into the darkness before the farmer could get off another round in their direction.

A year later, the United States by then well engaged in a vicious overseas war with Germany, no one went riding in String Prairie on New Year's Eve.

THE NIGHT THEY BARBECUED BEVO

One of the more bizarre events in Texas collegiate history took place in Austin on a January night in 1920. The occasion was a tribute to Bevo, the University of Texas's longhorn mascot. More than two hundred "wearers of the T" and their guests attended a feed at the men's gymnasium in the steer's honor.

The UT football team had been called the Longhorns since 1904, but another twelve years went by before an orange-blooded alum (class of '11) decided the school needed a flesh-and-blood longhorn stomping around on the sidelines during football games.

Steve Pinckney, referred to in one newspaper account as "the grandfather of the Longhorn steer," collected a dollar each from 124 UT graduates to buy the brute. The transaction occurred in the Panhandle, where the seller loaded the longhorn onto a railroad cattle car for shipment to Austin.

The first Bevo had a hard life—stolen, branded 13–0 and, finally, barbecued. *Author's collection.*

This longhorn already had an impressive history. The steer had been captured by a posse of Texans in a raid on Mexican cattle rustlers near Laredo in the fall of 1916. Presumably, the animal had been stolen from the Texas side of the river sometime prior to his repatriation.

Pinckney presented the well-traveled steer to the UT student body on Thanksgiving Day 1916. The two-legged Longhorns went on to defeat Texas A&M 22–7, avenging a devastating 13–0 loss to the Aggies the year before.

For a time there was talk of branding the steer with a big T and the numbers 22–7, but the notion got overridden as unnecessarily cruel. The holidays came and went, and then it was February. On the morning of February 11, 1917, the owner of the stockyard where the longhorn was kept made a startling discovery: intruders, presumably Aggies, had slipped up on the penned mascot and used a red-hot running iron to sear the 13–0 score from 1915 on the steer's flank.

The steer's embarrassed student handlers, in turn, soon came up with a clever way to save face for their school, though it was a little hard on their mascot. Students converted the 13 into a "B," the hyphen into an "E" and inserted a "V" in front of the zero. That spelled Bevo, the brand name of a popular near beer.

At least that's the story that both UT and Texas A&M accepted for years in regard to how Bevo got his name. Alas, more recent research has shown that Bevo had his name before the Aggie branding incident. Indeed, in an article on the steer in the December 1916 *Alcalde*, a UT alumni magazine, the editor proclaimed: "His name is Bevo. Long may he reign!"

The generally accepted theory today is that Bevo does not honor a long-forgotten alcohol-free beer but resulted from a then-current fad inspired by a popular newspaper comic strip in which nicknames were often created by adding an "o" to a character trait or other description, as in "Beeve" shortened to Bevo.

However Bevo got his name, it was ancient history three years later when UT students and supporters gathered to honor their Aggie-branded mascot. Dr. Charles W. Ramsdell, master of ceremonies at the event, introduced Dr. Robert E. Vinson, president of UT. Vinson went on to give a flag-waving oration concerning "the qualities of the true American citizen."

Though the university faculty was doing its best, in Vinson's judgment, civilization "thus far has failed to develop to the fullest the three essentials of true manhood and womanhood—the spirit, the mind, and the body." As perhaps only a highly educated academician could do, the UT president came up with a way to claim that Bevo "typified all three qualities." Dropping the bull metaphor, he concluded his remarks with the assertion that "education should broaden the student in all three essentials."

Next to speak was Pinckney, who related the steer's colorful pedigree. He was followed by Tom Inglehart, Bevo's custodian for the past three years. Finally, fittingly named Alfred Bull stood to tell how Bevo got his name. After that, the celebrants were treated to rope tricks, a wild Indian act and music.

Where was Bevo while all the speechifying in his honor went on? Well, to paraphrase the modern beef industry, Bevo…he's what's for dinner.

The headline in the next day's Austin newspaper pretty well summed it up: "Famous Longhorn Steer Is Eaten by Varsity Students: Bevo of Fond, but Sometimes Unpleasant, Memories, Served at Barbeque." The newspaper story went on to say that the demise of the steer (why Bevo was available to barbecue was not explained) marked the end of a tradition, which just goes to show the importance of not believing everything you read in the newspapers.

Bevo I's successor, Bevo XIV, currently presides as one of college football's most notable mascots. But so far as is known, the gathering that winter evening in 1920 marked the only time Bevo ended up in a barbecue pit.

ABOUT THE AUTHOR

An elected member of the Texas Institute of Letters, Mike Cox is the author of more than twenty nonfiction books, as well as hundreds of articles and essays, over a writing career spanning more than forty years.

In September 2011, at the West Texas Book Festival in Abilene, he was recognized with the A.C. Greene Award for lifetime achievement.

His best-selling work has been a two-volume, 250,000-word history of the Texas Rangers, *Wearing the Cinco Peso: The Texas Rangers 1821–1900* and *Time of the Rangers: The Texas Rangers 1900–Present*, published in 2008 and 2009.

A former award-winning reporter, Cox was a longtime spokesman for the Texas Department of Public Safety and later communications manager for the Texas Department of Transportation before retiring in 2007. He retired from retirement in 2010 to go back to work for the state as a spokesman for the Texas Parks and Wildlife Department.

When not working or writing, he spends as much time as he can fishing and hunting. He lives in Fredricksburg in the Texas hill country.

Visit us at
www.historypress.net

CPSIA information can be obtained
at www.ICGtesting.com
Printed in the USA
LVHW081559121021
700234LV00002B/188